The
SUPERNATURAL
Guide to
THE OTHER
SIDE

Interpret signs,
communicate *with*
spirits, *and* uncover
the secrets of the
afterlife

Adams Media
New York   London   Toronto   Sydney   New Delhi

Adams Media
An Imprint of Simon & Schuster, Inc.
57 Littlefield Street
Avon, Massachusetts 02322

First Adams Media trade paperback edition AUGUST 2017

ADAMS MEDIA and colophon are trademarks of Simon and Schuster.

For information about special discounts for bulk purchases, please contact Simon & Schuster Special Sales at 1-866-506-1949 or business@simonandschuster.com.

The Simon & Schuster Speakers Bureau can bring authors to your live event. For more information or to book an event contact the Simon & Schuster Speakers Bureau at 1-866-248-3049 or visit our website at www.simonspeakers.com.

Interior design by Heather McKiel
Interior images © 123RF

Manufactured in the United States of America

10 9 8 7 6 5 4 3 2 1

Library of Congress Cataloging-in-Publication Data has been applied for.

ISBN 978-1-5072-0430-6
ISBN 978-1-5072-0431-3 (ebook)

Contains material adapted from the following titles published by Adams Media, an Imprint of Simon & Schuster, Inc.: *The Everything® Ghost Hunting Book, 2nd Edition* by Melissa Martin Ellis, copyright © 2014, ISBN 978-1-4405-7147-3; *The Everything® Guide to Evidence of the Afterlife* by Joseph M. Higgins and Chuck Bergman, copyright © 2011, ISBN 978-1-4405-1008-3; *How to Be a Psychic* by Michael R. Hathaway, copyright © 2017, ISBN 978-1-5072-0061-2; and *How to Interpret Dreams* by Adams Media, copyright © 2017, ISBN 978-1-5072-0190-9.

Contents

Introduction

Have you heard a song on the radio and wondered if a deceased loved one was trying to tell you something? Have you seen a cardinal and wondered if it was a sign from the other side? Do you have vivid dreams that feature deceased relatives? These common occurrences show how a person's soul might be able to separate from his or her physical body and continue after "life" as we know it on earth.

From seemingly coincidental events that are just too meaningful to happen by chance, to paranormal phenomena such as ghosts, to near-death experiences, today, more than ever before, people are talking openly about these happenings in their daily lives. You, too, have the power to invite these connections into your life.

Through modern scientific technology, researchers have opened the door to new possibilities of the existence of another realm beyond the physical plane that is seen by the world today. The study of consciousness has shown the possibility of life continuing after death. Recent scientific advances have revolutionized ideas about what everything is made of, including man himself. The possibility of multiple dimensions interacting with this one is no longer science fiction, but on the verge of becoming reality.

Interacting with those on the other side does not have to eliminate or clash with your current belief system. It can coexist with the faith or cultural beliefs you have followed throughout your life. Judge the evidence with an open mind, accept what you can, and contemplate the rest.

The Supernatural Guide to the Other Side brings you up-to-date studies, theories, and evidence of the afterlife, and teaches you what to make of these signs and signals you see—and how to be open to receiving more of them. You will be asked to open your mind to new possibilities. As the evidence is presented, ask yourself the question that French philosopher and Jesuit priest Pierre Teilhard de Chardin posed ages ago: Are you a human being having a spiritual experience, or a spiritual being having a human experience?

PART 1

Afterlife Basics

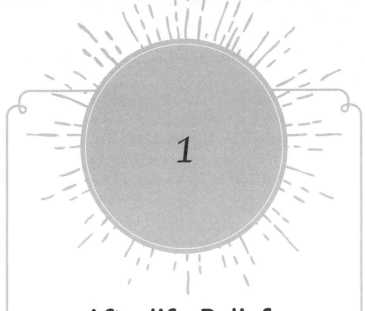

Afterlife Beliefs in Ancient and Modern Cultures

Cultural beliefs in the afterlife have had a great influence on organized religions. Many afterlife theories and concepts have transcended regional cultures and become the foundations of modern religious belief systems. From the earliest days of the ancient Greek and Chinese cultures, you will find many similarities to modern-day thought concerning the afterlife.

Cultural Beliefs Across the Globe

As we can tell from ancient cave paintings, man has always found the idea of an afterlife to be not only interesting but also something that is a part of him. Human beings have a self-awareness that other species lack, and this includes awareness of the eventual death of the physical body. Some of the modern-day phenomena, such as near-death experiences and deathbed visitations, also took place thousands of years ago. This led individuals to question if there was more to their existence than what they could observe. All the great civilizations of the past have had some belief in an afterlife.

EGYPTIAN MYTHOLOGY

The highlight of an ancient Egyptian's life was ultimately his death and burial. The Egyptians believed in an eternal afterlife, complete with possession of their earthly riches. In their overwhelming desire to secure a perpetual place in the afterlife, much time, effort, and thought was put toward preparing for death. One of the most important aspects of their belief system was the idea that if the soul were to live on in the afterlife, a person's body had to remain relatively intact.

The ancient Egyptians assured their place in the afterlife through:

- **Mummification:** The body and the internal organs would be preserved and embalmed separately.
- **Protecting the body:** The body would be entombed and therefore safe from harm.
- **Nourishment:** The deceased would receive regular offerings of food and drink, or illustrations of them, in the tomb.

Inscriptions and illustrations describing the occupant's life were made on the tomb. Inside the tomb there were also various amulets of a protective nature, a decorated coffin, and sometimes a stone or wooden sarcophagus, inside which the mummy was placed.

After undertaking the perilous journey through the underworld, contending with creatures, gods, and gatekeepers, the deceased faced his day of judgment. Anubis, the god of the dead, led the soul to the Hall of Two Truths, where the deceased stood in front of forty-two divine judges.

Once the soul passed this test, he was led to a set of scales, where his heart, containing the deeds of his lifetime, was weighed against the feather of truth, belonging to the goddess Ma'at. If the heart was found to be heavier than the feather, the soul was fed to the god Ammit, the "Devourer," and the soul was condemned to remain in the underworld forever. However, if the heart was lighter than the feather, or the scales were balanced, the deceased had passed the final test and was given over to Osiris, the god of the underworld and chief judge, who welcomed him into the afterlife, the Field of Rushes.

In this beautiful world the real life of the deceased was mirrored, but with none of his earthly problems—there was only happiness. The afterlife was seen as a perfect existence in an ideal version of Egypt.

ANCIENT CHINESE AFTERLIFE BELIEFS

The ancient Chinese had a unique perspective on the afterlife, which underwent a great change with the rise of Buddhism in China. The Chinese Taoists were greatly concerned with life after death and the survival of an individual's soul even after his physical demise.

Chinese metaphysical philosophy teaches that each human being is an amalgamation of two souls, the yin and yang. These are together during the lifetime of an individual, but at the time of death, the two souls separate and go in different directions. This is in harmony with the cosmos, which was also created after the integration of light and dark, the yin and yang elements.

Kuei and *shen* represent the two extremes, the lower dark and evil element and the higher spiritual element. The ancient Chinese idea of the soul was dualistic. The *po* was an earth soul that came into existence at the time of conception, while the *hun* was made of chi, the life force, and came into existence at the time of birth. Each soul had its own after-life: While the *hun* went to heaven or a special underworld, the *po* went to the darker realms of the cosmos.

The concept of heaven as the dwelling place of gods is also a very old Chinese notion. According to the Shang Dynasty beliefs, heaven was also the place where the *hun* (the good soul) would go. However, only the powerful *hun*, those of earthly kings, could enter heaven; the rest would be given a place lower than heaven or would be reincarnated with a longer life span.

Though not clearly defined, the Chinese notion of the underworld, the Yellow Springs, could be conceived of as hell. It was the destination of the evil souls, the *po*. Yellow Springs was a miserable place where the souls were punished for their bad deeds.

DEATH, BURIAL, AND THE AFTERLIFE IN GREECE

The Greeks believed that when a person dies, his spirit or psyche leaves the physical body in the form of a little breath or puff of air. The dead body was washed, anointed with oil, and dressed for the rituals:

1. **Prosthesis:** This refers to the laying out and display of the body so relatives, friends, and acquaintances could come and pay their respects to the deceased.

2. **Ekphora:** Ekphora is the funeral procession, where the deceased was brought to the cemetery for burial. Ekphora usually took place just before dawn, and it involved building the funeral pyre (if the dead body was to be burned) or filling up the grave with objects of daily use.

3. **Interment:** The remains of the body, or ashes, if cremated, were placed inside the tomb specially built for the deceased. Immortality lay in the continued remembrance of the deceased person by his family members.

In Greece, it was believed that all souls, whether good or bad, go to the underworld realm, Hades, the land of the dead. Tartaros was an area below Hades, where disobedient and evil spirits were punished. Elysium was a beautiful and tranquil place, inhabited by good spirits. When the concept of reward and punishment was introduced in the postclassical period, Tartaros became hell and Elysium became heaven. The Greeks believed those who were not buried or cremated in the appropriate manner would be destined to suffer between the two worlds and would not be given an entry into the land of the dead until these rites were completed.

When the hour of death arrived, red-robed deities came to take the spirit of the deceased to the land of the dead. To reach the land of the dead they had to cross Acheron, one of the five underground rivers. Charon, the ferryman, took the spirits of the dead to the other end of the river. Charon demanded a small coin (*obol*) for this service; this is why the dead were buried with a coin in their mouth.

After crossing Acheron, the soul of the deceased was judged by Hades, the god of the underworld, and all the sons of Zeus. The deceased was assigned an eternal home depending on the deeds and the kind of life he lived:

- **Ordinary souls:** Neutral regions of Hades, a dull and drab place
- **Evil souls (those who committed many crimes):** Tartaros (hell)
- **Pure and blessed souls:** Elysium (heaven)

All the burial rituals and beliefs of the ancient Greeks point to the fact that they were fascinated by the concept of the afterlife.

DEATH AND BURIAL IN THE ROMAN CULTURE

Romans could either bury or burn their dead, depending upon the personal customs. The Romans believed the soul of a deceased person could only find peace when the physical body was prepared in a proper manner and all ceremonies were conducted appropriately. If this was not done, the soul would haunt its home and other family members.

Ancient Romans believed that depending on the deeds performed in the mortal world, the soul was assigned an afterlife in either hell or heaven. Hell was a location where those who committed serious sins would be punished. The punishment was in the form of fire and endless pain and suffering.

Just like the Greeks, the Romans believed that the soul of the deceased person was carried to the other end of the world by crossing a river. They believed that three judges—Minos, Rhadamanthus, and Aeacus—took an account of the deceased's life and activities and assigned an afterlife for the soul:

- Warriors and heroes were sent to Elysium (heaven).
- Good and honest citizens were sent to the Plain of Asphodel.
- Evil spirits, those that had offended the gods, were sent to Tartaros (hell).

EARLY CELTIC BELIEFS

The early Celts were a diverse group of tribes that were spread across Gaul, Britain, Ireland, Asia Minor, Central Europe, and the Balkans. The Celtic people practiced Druidism, a religion overseen by priests and priestesses called Druids. For Celts, the afterlife was as real as the mortal world. After a person's death, her soul needed a clear path so it could travel to the otherworld, which is why all windows and doors were kept wide open when a person died.

In the Druidism culture, a priest would come and explain to the dying person how her soul would travel to its final destination and find eternal peace in the otherworld. In the case of sudden death, the priest would come and whisper this information to the deceased. Souls that did not get proper religious direction became targets for evil spirits, or were left to roam around restlessly, causing trouble for the living.

After the mourning period, there was a funeral feast. A part of the food was given to the deceased person as "grave food" before the body was finally buried or cremated. The Celts preferred burial to cremation, especially for great warriors, noblemen, and leaders. Mounts and tombs were built for such people; for everyday people, normal graves were dug. With each body, objects of daily use, personal belongings, and food were also placed inside the grave. Finally, on the seventh day, the body would be buried or burned per the tribal customs.

THE WAKE

The wake refers to the period during which the body of the deceased was laid out after the soul reached its afterlife. The body was washed with the waters from a sacred well to keep it protected and was wrapped in the *Eslene* (death cloth). It was then placed in a coffin in the center of the house, where mourners could come and pay their respects. During the wake, mourners would come and sit by the corpse and share memories of the deceased.

Druids believed that the soul was reincarnated as another entity in the living world, either as a plant or animal, or again as a human. When one gained complete understanding of the immortality of the soul and the process of rebirth, she would be moved to a higher realm of existence, a different outer world. This would continue until the soul reached the highest state, "the source," after which the soul would be eternally rested.

NATIVE AMERICAN RITUALS AND CEREMONIES

A common theme found in Native American spirituality is the idea of finding god in nature. From hunting, Native Americans developed a belief in animism, the idea that spirits exist in all natural objects, creatures, and phenomena, including animals. Farming brought forth food and medicine, and taught a respect for Gaia, the Earth Mother (a living, breathing, conscious being), who provided for her children. Shamans, the medicine men of the societies, helped give these spiritual forces meaning and used them for healing practices. Their understanding of the afterlife was that the spirit divided into two parts: the organic that returned to the Mother and the spirit that returned to the Father.

Indigenous belief systems vary from tribe to tribe. The following are some common themes in Native American spirituality, as illustrated through the Oglala Lakota perspective:

- *Wakan tanka*—Literally translated as "great mystery." It's considered the source, the creator of all, "the Great and Incomprehensible One." This name expresses the idea that humans are incapable of ever truly comprehending the ways of the Great Spirit.

- *Topa olowan*—A complex ideology that recognizes the sacred four directions of north, south, east, and west as sentient beings that guard the four quarters of the world.

- *Ina maka*—This term translates as "mother earth."

Religious Beliefs and Theories of the Afterlife

The origins of organized religions date back a few thousands years. The possibility of life after death has always been a subject of interest for many, spurring long, heated debates among philosophers and theologians.

CHRISTIANITY

Christianity, a monotheistic religion, can be broken up into many different denominations. Catholicism, Protestantism, and Eastern Orthodoxy are the largest, and they have similarities and differences in their theories of the afterlife. Most Christians believe in an afterlife, described as heaven and hell. Heaven is a beautiful paradise where souls reside with God and enjoy all his love and support. The opposite is hell, a place lacking any presence of God or his love.

Catholicism

The afterlife belief of this denomination starts with the concept of baptism. The sacrament of baptism represents the acceptance of Jesus as your savior, and allows you the opportunity to enter into heaven when it is time for you to cross to the other side. Once considered a physical place, heaven is now accepted as an eternal relationship with God.

If one commits a mortal sin and does not confess and repent that sin, he will go to hell. Once believed to be a place of eternal fire and torment, hell is now considered "the pain, frustration, and emptiness of life without God," according to the Catholic Church. The Catholic Church also believes in a realm called purgatory. Pope John Paul II explained that physical integrity is necessary to enter into perfect communion with God; therefore, "the term purgatory does not indicate a place, but a condition of existence," where Christ "removes . . . the remnants of imperfection."

Protestantism

Protestantism encompasses a group of Christian denominations that separated from the Catholic Church during the sixteenth-century

Reformation. Their concerns about how one gets into heaven forged their move to independence; for example, they believed that one could enter heaven through faith alone, and only Christ could forgive sins. There is no purgatory, as in the Catholic Church, where souls need to be purified before entering heaven. Faith, a gift from God, is their salvation. The Bible is the most important basis for the Protestant Church, and it is the final word for all practices and beliefs.

A difference of opinion has emerged between the conservative and liberal wings of many Protestant denominations. The conservatives believe in a literal place of hell, while the more liberal tend to believe that a loving God could not put people into such a place of torment. They feel it is more likely an eternity separated from God himself.

Eastern Orthodox

The Eastern and Western Churches split in the eleventh century over a disagreement about the authority of the pope. The Eastern Churches denied the authority of the pope. Eastern Orthodox beliefs teach that after the soul leaves the body there is an anticipation of judgment. This occurs either in heaven, where there is a sense of light, or in hell, where there is a sense of darkness. On Judgment Day, the body is reunited with the soul to fully experience heaven or hell.

JUDAISM

Judaism is one of the oldest world religions, believed to have originated around 2000 B.C.E. It is an Abrahamic religion; that is, Abraham is its patriarch. Judaism teaches that death is not the end of one's being, and primarily focuses on life now rather than the life to come. A person's current actions are more important than the beliefs in *olam ha-ba*, the afterlife. The Torah, the most important Jewish text, establishes the laws Jews live by and is said to show the believer the path to salvation.

The Torah speaks of the equal and just consequences for all actions within the life span of earthly beings. This focus on the balancing of bad deeds with punishment and good deeds with rewards within a lifetime precludes any specific detailed mention of death and events of the afterlife, according to some scholars. However, others believe that these messages are simply concealed and become apparent when interpreted correctly. The widely accepted belief is that the good will be happy in company of loved ones until the arrival of the Messiah, when the soul is resurrected, while the bad will not receive this grace. The different movements of Judaism have varying thoughts concerning the afterlife, but these are all speculative. They consider it a distraction to focus on the afterlife, instead placing their attention on their daily lives.

The Afterlife in Judaism

The concept of afterlife is contained in the Talmud, which comprises the Mishnah (written text of the Oral Commandments) and Gemara (interpretation of the Commandments). The journey of the deceased is described in this Scripture in detail.

When a person dies, his soul is brought for judgment. Those who have never swerved from the teachings of the Scriptures and have led a pure life are ushered into the *olam ha-ba*, or world to come.

The unrighteous go to a place referred to as *sheol* after death. The earth splits apart to swallow these souls and send them to *sheol*. Here the soul may be given a chance to review past actions and gain an understanding of how much wrong it has committed. Through this process, the soul gains wisdom. Some believe this one-year period is set aside for punishment for bad deeds during life. At the end, the soul is elevated to a higher plane and can move on to the world to come.

Resurrection

Rambam's Thirteen Principles of Faith speaks about resurrection. According to this concept, when the Messiah arrives, he will create the perfect world, or the world to come. The good souls awaiting resurrection in paradise will be given a new life in this world of peace and happiness so that they can enjoy the fruits of their good deeds.

Some followers of Judaism hold that the process of rebirth is a continuous one, and the righteous souls are sent back to earth to help make it a better place. Still others believe that only souls that have yet to complete earthly duties are reincarnated so that they may have a second chance to finish their work.

ISLAM

The concept of an afterlife plays an extremely important role in Islam and governs, to a large extent, the Islamic way of life. According to the Koran, the very purpose of life is to live in a way that is pleasing to God (Allah) so that one may achieve paradise in the afterlife. Followers of Islam believe that an account of each person's good and bad deeds is opened at the time of puberty, and this record is used to determine the person's fate in the afterlife.

The Koran, God's words to Muhammad, is the holy book of Islam and is meant as guidance to Muslims and others who wish to learn the meanings of Islam. It clearly states that people should live their lives in a certain way if they want to live a good afterlife. Although this concept of actions (in the current life) and reward (heaven or hell in the afterlife) is present in many religions, the impact that it has on Muslims is much greater than in any other religion.

Islam incorporates the concept of a soul. Each person is considered the combination of a body and soul. Similar to the Judeo-Christian tradition, the idea that a physical body is needed for life after death is also present in Islam. The Koran speaks of the Day of Reckoning or the Day of Resurrection (*Yawm al-Qiyamah*), when the dead will be resurrected and given an afterlife according to their deeds.

COMMUNICATING WITH SPIRITS

According to Mirza Tahir Ahmad, a famous Muslim scholar and a caliph of the Ahmadiyya Muslim Community, the belief that spirits can return and can communicate with the living is incorrect. He pointed out that according to the Koran, it is completely forbidden for a spirit that has left this world to return to it, and that there is no way you can summon a spirit to visit you. However, he emphasized that communication with spirits is possible through mediums like prayer and dreams, and that it has been observed many times in the past, as well as mentioned in the Koran.

Afterlife Before Resurrection

Muslims believe that for a spirit, the period after the death of a person and before the Day of Resurrection is like the period spent by an unborn child in the womb. The Resurrection is thus the second birth of a spirit, but it takes place after an extremely long period. During this period, the spirit's level of consciousness increases. As the Day of Resurrection comes closer, this embryo (spirit) becomes more and more peaceful and blissful if it is supposed to go to heaven, and it becomes more and more impatient if it is supposed to go to hell.

Afterlife after Resurrection

The Koran also speaks about the specific nature of heaven and hell. According to the Koran, paradise, also called "the Garden" (*Janna*), is a place of physical and spiritual pleasure, with lofty mansions (39:20), delicious food and drink (52:22), and virgin companions called *houris* (56:17–19). There are seven heavens (17:46).

Hell is mentioned as having seven doors (39:71, 15:43), and the Koran states, "The unbelievers among the People of the Book and the pagans shall burn forever in the fire of Hell. They are the vilest of all creatures" (98:1–8).

HINDUISM

Hinduism adheres to the principle of an afterlife. Death is seen not as the end, but rather as the beginning of a new life. The idea of transmigration is broadly classified into two major categories: *linear*, the belief that a human is born only once and after death is judged on the basis of his deeds, and *cyclical*, wherein an individual's soul is reborn as a new human being and the deeds of the past life are carried into the next.

The *atman* is the soul of a human being, or the "true self," and it exists without any form. When you are born, a soul is transferred into your body in the form of life, and when you have completed your life in the physical world, your *atman* leaves your body. *Atman* is pure and is the essence of divinity. Each human being is connected to the Supreme Being through his soul. Just like energy, the *atman* can neither be created nor destroyed and is immortal. It keeps moving from one body to another until it finally comes together with God.

Karma

Karma is the act or deed that runs the circle of cause and effect called *samsara*. Karma is the infrastructure put in place by God to keep a check on the deeds of human beings, whether good or evil. Your fortune and misfortune are a result of your karma, and it takes into account not only your present life but your past life karmas as well.

Karma can be good or bad based on the actions of a human being. Good deeds are rewarded and bring you closer to God, but bad karma takes you away from God and puts you back into the pattern of birth, death, and rebirth.

Moksha means "liberation" in Sanskrit, and is described as the state when the *atman* gains salvation. When God liberates a soul from the wheel of karma and merges it with himself, the *atman* achieves *moksha*. Ultimately, good or bad karma will determine how and if you will get out of the "wheel of life" and finally merge with God for eternity in the afterlife.

BUDDHISM

Buddhism holds the view that life on earth is the embodiment of suffering and that people will undergo multiple reincarnations based on how morally and justly they lived their previous lives. However, whereas other world religions have a very clearly defined and ordered body of moral law designed to regulate human conduct, Buddhism instead identifies the notion of desire as the root of all problems. It is believed that the coveting of anything in the world—whether material or sexual— brings pain and suffering.

Buddhism and Its Views on the Afterlife

Buddhists do not believe in the concept of a soul per se, and so they use the word *anatta* to embody their firm view that all things in existence are transitory. Because all things are in a state of constant flux, there is no concept of immortality within Buddhism.

The countless negative emotions that we face in our daily lives, such as disappointment, frustration, and anger, are a result of our ignorance of the law of nature, which is "impermanence." Nothing in this world remains constant or forever, and to get rid of our sorrows we need to understand this fully.

Nirvana/Nibbana

Another fundamental precept of Buddhism related to the afterlife is that the attainment of perfection, the liberation from the pain and suffering of our stressful existences, is achieved through nirvana. Nirvana is the achievement of total oblivion, the extinction of a person both as an entity as well as a concept. Nirvana refers to the state of purity, a mental state where all desires, selfishness, greed, and anger have been extinguished and eliminated.

There is a clearly defined process within Buddhism of the various channels of the afterlife. Whenever a person's physical being comes to an end through death, his spirit will then endure a process that lasts for forty-nine days called the *bardo*. During this time there will be one of two possible outcomes:

1. The spirit of the deceased person will be promptly returned to earth in order to recommence the cycle of birth, suffering, and death.
2. The spirit of the deceased person will reach a level of enlightenment so as to entitle him to reach the ultimate goal of nirvana.

At the initial stage of the *bardo* process, commonly referred to as the *chikai bardo*, the deceased person will come to the realization that he has indeed died and that his soul has been duly separated from his physical body.

During the second stage of the *bardo* process, commonly referred to as the *chonyid bardo*, the spirit of the deceased person will have to face a number of distressing visualizations that will appear before him, which are the physical embodiments of his actions during his time on earth.

GNOSTICISM

Gnostics have a unique religious belief that knowledge is salvation. This does not denote knowledge of the material world but that of spiritual reality and an understanding of the cosmos. The discovery of a collection of Gnostic texts near Nag Hammadi, Egypt, in 1945 led to the belief that Gnostics learned the principles of their religion directly from Christ's disciples.

According to Gnosticism, all humankind was created by Demiurge, a deity that has a dualistic nature—a physical form and a divine spark, which lies within. Those who have not gleaned the supreme knowledge continue to move toward Demiurge's Garden of Delights — condemning their divine spark to lie concealed, even after death.

Salvation signifies the release of the divine spark from its physical bondage to merge with the supreme God at death instead of being reincarnated. This salvation can be attained through gnosis, or knowledge. According to the Gnostic Gospel of Thomas, Jesus explains that humans must comprehend the supreme God while on earth in order to gain salvation at death. The physical body of a being who has failed to complete the work of gnosis is destroyed at death, and the divine spark is transferred to another body to remain on earth in search of the true knowledge. This cycle continues until the being achieves gnosis.

MYSTICISM

Mysticism has found a place in many religions across the world. The mystic school of thought holds that it is every living being's eternal quest to find the pathways and processes to attain the ultimate goal of reunion with a supreme power. Different mystic forms of religions describe this ultimate salvation in different ways.

Mystic Christians

Mystic Christians believe that enlightened souls attain the final goal of oneness with Christ by becoming Christ. The underlying belief is that through prayer and devotion it is possible in time to elevate the soul to a higher plane. In this plane, the soul achieves union with the essence of God.

Kabbalistic Judaism

Flavius Josephus, a first-century Jewish historian, stated that the souls of the evil are punished in the afterlife, while good souls are given a new life in a physical form on earth. According to the Zohar, a religious text of kabbalistic Jews, the evildoers are consigned to resurrections on earth after memories of previous births and actions are erased. These souls must rectify past wrongs in the reincarnated life to attain salvation.

Sufism

In Sufism, or Islamic mysticism, God assesses all souls on the Day of Judgment, or *Yawm ad-Din*. Those who have surrendered themselves to the belief and practice of worshipping God will be granted a place in paradise (*janna*), while nonbelievers will be sent to hell (*jahannam*). As opposed to traditional Muslims, Sufis believe that paradise brings them closest to the Supreme Being and lifts the veil between the souls and Allah. In this way, they are reunited with the Supreme Being to become one with him.

UNIVERSALISM

In his position paper entitled "Universalism and the Bible," Yale philosopher and researcher Keith DeRose defines Universalism as "the position that eventually all human beings will be saved and will enjoy everlasting life with Christ." DeRose cites various biblical verses found in the New Testament that use the word *all* in reference to who will be saved in the afterlife. He maintains that you don't have to be a Christian or believe in Christ to be saved, because the Scriptures make no distinction as to who Christ will save. For some, "all" may even include the devil.

While some Universalists believe in punishment or retribution in the afterlife, they maintain that any punishment will not last forever, although the Bible speaks of "eternal" punishment. They explain that the Bible's original Greek text used the word *aionios*, which means "age enduring" or "pertaining to an age," and took a different interpretation when it was translated into English as "eternal."

WICCA

Well-known Wiccan author Gary Cantrell explains that Wicca is based on "harmony with nature and all aspects of the God and Goddesses divinity." Wiccans believe in the Threefold Law, which says that all the good you do will return to you threefold in this life. Conversely, all the harm that you do will return to you threefold as well. This law of cause and effect is viewed not as punishment but as a natural result of your action. It may come before death or even soon after the action is done.

Wiccans also believe that all souls go to a place called Summerland after death, where you can meet those who have gone before. Summerland is pictured as a place of beauty and peace, where you can see and experience all that you hold close to your heart in full beauty for eternity. It is not a place of judgment but rather a place of self-evaluation where your soul can review the past life and gain an understanding of its total impact on the world. Only after learning your lesson in Summerland will your soul be reincarnated so you can try anew, although you won't be able to remember Summerland when you reach the physical plane again.

SPIRITUALISM

"Thinking about death and dying can be morbid, unless you believe in an afterlife that has meaning," says ordained spiritualist minister Joanna Bartlett-Gustina in her article "What Spiritualism Teaches About Death." Spiritualism maintains that your spirit survives death and can communicate with the living through a third party, usually a medium or spiritualist minister. This interaction of the dead with the living is based on the idea that the dead are able to observe the living from a distance and often want to give knowledge and advice to living friends and relatives through a medium.

Death is viewed not as the end but as a transition from one state of awareness to another. While spiritualists believe in life after death, they do not propose places of punishment and reward such as a heaven and hell.

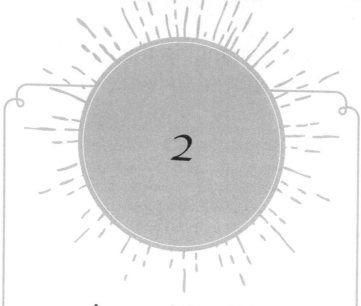

Is an Afterlife Really Possible?

The concept of an afterlife doesn't always neatly fit into traditional scientific research. Yet recent astounding discoveries pertaining to physical matter have revealed the possibility that there is more to the physical world than we can see. While classic physics has been the accepted science for the explanations of how large objects interact with one another, quantum physics looks at how things react at the smallest subatomic levels. Quantum physics can ponder the possibility of an afterlife from a purely scientific point of view, and this field is bringing spirituality and science closer together.

Understanding the Fabric
of the Universe

The traditional common sense view of reality is based on the belief that the things that we experience in the world exist objectively and independently in relation to us. We assume that what we're able to see, hear, taste, smell, or touch actually exists as an independent reality.

Now consider the subatomic world of quantum physics. Quantum physics describes the world of microscopic phenomena, a world of electrons, photons, and atoms. It assumes a worldview in which classical rules of physics do not apply, a world where quantum entanglements, coherences, tunnels, and probabilities hold sway for subatomic particles and energy waves. Basically, it's the small stuff—the really small stuff—that makes up everything. This world of the tiny subatomic stuff, which makes up the big stuff like cars, buildings, and galaxies, has its own set of rules that are drastically different from the large-object world you experience in your daily life. Not only does this quantum world play by a different rulebook, but also you, as an observer, have much to do with the manifestation of the reality you are observing.

The underlying subatomic fabric does not behave in a way that our minds can easily understand. For instance, a subatomic object appears to have properties of both a particle with mass and a wave (e.g., a sound wave) with energy. The way an individual will see a subatomic object, as particle or wave, depends on how the individual constructs the experiment. But when you're not observing it, any subatomic object exists in a stable and undefined state. Fixed points of reality do not really exist in the pre-observational subatomic world. When an observation is made, the object "actualizes" by collapsing into one of the many forms dictated by its probability wave, and the particle appears to come into being in that instant. So in reality nothing exists until you look at it.

If we could observe an electron's movements through time, what we would see is a discrete energy bundle that appears to jump in an irregular series of seemingly random leaps, collapsing from wave to matter and just as quickly disappearing again into another wave. These particles would seem to flash in and out of existence before our eyes with such rapidity that they might appear like a cloud.

The human body is also made of this small stuff. However, an electron really has no path, no exact location, and no exact momentum. Our observation freezes one of those potentialities in time, causing it to become real. Where the object appears next can't be known with certainty; it can only be expressed as a probability. These possibilities could open up our definition of who we really are and how we might create our own existence, now and in the afterlife.

Heisenberg's Uncertainty Principle

In 1927, while working at the Institute for Theoretical Physics at the University of Copenhagen, now known as the Niels Bohr Institute, German physicist Werner Heisenberg published a groundbreaking theory of quantum mechanics that provided a new way of thinking about atomic interactions, and a new way of looking at the world.

His theories resulted in a major shift in how scientists think about the nature of reality itself. The Heisenberg uncertainty principle tells us that we cannot exactly determine both the position and momentum of a subatomic particle at the same time. The reason for this is simply that watching requires an energy intermediary, such as a photon of light, to interact with what we are observing, and in the subatomic world, that interaction can change the makeup of the observed particle. According to Heisenberg, "the path comes into existence only when we observe it." And this is not predictable using the classical mechanics of physics.

THE CLASSICAL UNDERSTANDING

In the common day-to-day world, all large objects appear to be fixed things that exist even if no one is there to observe them. It's commonly understood that you can measure objects, whether they are at rest or in motion, and you can make predictions as to exactly where they will be located based on that information. Radar and sonar work like this. That's how ships and airplanes can be tracked. In baseball you can measure a ball's mass, and if the ball is thrown through the air, you can determine its position and speed. If you wanted to you could apply the formulas of classical mechanics to accurately predict the exact spot where the ball will land. The foundation of this classical physics was first published by Sir Isaac Newton in the *Principia*, three books that are regarded as some of the most important works in the history of science. As long as we limited our observations to large objects, Newtonian physics won.

Have you thought about how you can see a ball in a mechanical sense? Assume it is a night game and the source of illumination is light rays from the lights above the field. These light rays (also known as *photons*) are constantly hitting that ball. Some of these photons will bounce off the ball and reflect into your eyes, and the ball appears to move in an uninterrupted and expected direction. The classical world is predictable and behaves as expected, until the outfielder drops the ball . . . but that's another story.

APPLYING HEISENBERG'S UNCERTAINTY PRINCIPLE

In the Heisenberg model, the underlying subatomic fabric of the world behaves in a way that cannot easily be understood. Fixed points of reality do not seem to pre-exist in the subatomic world; only quantum probabilities with inherent uncertainties and inaccuracy exist. And it is only when you make an observation that these probabilities collapse into an observed reality.

STRING THEORY

According to string theory, the fundamental building blocks of nature are tiny strings (much smaller than observable subatomic particles). These strings manifest as different particles only because of their different vibrations. A possibility within string theory is that there is a huge number of universes that coexist with this universe, and these universes have their own space and time. Once scientists are able to construct reliable experiments to test string theory, concrete evidence of the afterlife is also likely to emerge. In fact, it could even help develop better means of communicating with dead people.

What these theories propose is that the things that make up a human being—matter and energy—can be interchangeable on a subatomic level. The afterlife could be the reconstructed form of an individual after the physical matter of the body dies.

Substances That Make Up a Physical Being

Quantum physics and biology are two fields of scientific study that have often been viewed as unrelated branches of knowledge. But is that separation accurate? In the past century, biology and the life sciences have made remarkable strides in understanding various cell processes, and this came about primarily through the study of molecular cell structures. However, there are many biological processes that are not yet completely understood. Could quantum mechanisms be responsible for some of the most inexplicable processes of life?

Even as the medical community tries to unravel the many mysteries of the human body (made up of atoms and subatomic particles), doctors and spiritualists have acknowledged the existence of an "energy field" around the human body. This energy field, or aura, extends externally and internally, interacting with everything around us. It comprises energy bodies that exist in succession and coexist in the same space.

ANOTHER TYPE OF SQUID

In the late twentieth century, scientists made the discovery that organs and tissues produce particular magnetic pulsations or biomagnetic fields. These can be measured using a superconducting quantum interference device (SQUID), which is a type of magnetometer and possibly the most sensitive measurement device known to humans. This discovery can be taken as proof of our existence beyond just the visible physical form.

It is also known through quantum physics that subatomic particles can phase in and out of existence, depending on the moment of observation. Quantum physics also explains that we are both particles (matter) and energy waves. The first law of thermodynamics says that energy cannot be created or destroyed, but only changed from one form to another. Therefore, a part of us must continue to exist after physical death, and perhaps this is a form we take in the afterlife.

It is believed that the human energy field is an instrument of wellness. Once disregarded by the medical community, alternate healing methods such as Reiki and therapeutic touch, a technique to stimulate energy fields, have become popular and accepted forms of treatment and have been shown to reduce postoperative recovery time.

DIFFERENT MODELS OF THE HUMAN ENERGY FIELD

One of the first references to the human energy field comes from the ancient Vedic traditions of India, which state that human beings exist on five *koshas* (layers/levels). The physical body is the outermost layer, followed by the energy body, which is the life force supporting the five senses. The third *kosha* is the mental body, where emotions and thoughts are processed. The next, the wisdom body, is a provider of intuition, helping humans reflect upon and evaluate the deeper meaning of life. Human consciousness is subtly manifested in the bliss body, which provides transcendental experiences.

Influential spiritual writer Alice Bailey (1880–1949) described human energy fields in relation to *chakras* and *nadis*. The literal translation of the Sanskrit word *chakra* is "spinning wheel." *Chakras* refer to energy centers, in the shape of rotating vortices, that serve as focal points for transmission and reception of energies. The human body is said to be composed of seven major *chakras* and a number of minor *chakras*. Every *chakra* spins at a different rate and absorbs those energies from the universal energy field that are harmonically related to its individual frequency. *Nadis* are channels or conduits that make up the subtle body. The vital force, or *prana*, flows through these *nadis*. According to Bailey, there are distinct human and spiritual energies that affect a person's life. The soul is said to express itself through four human mechanisms: the dense physical body, the etheric energy body, the emotional (astral) body, and the mental body.

World-renowned healer and bestselling author of *Hands of Light: A Guide to Healing Through the Human Energy Field*, Barbara Brennan, has described a seven-layer model of the human energy field, which is widely accepted by healers around the world.

SEVEN-LAYER MODEL OF THE HUMAN ENERGY FIELD

The seven-layer model is based on the three planes of existence: physical, astral, and spiritual. The physical plane consists of the physical body, thoughts, and emotions. On a higher plane of consciousness is the astral plane, which is composed of feelings and thoughts of humanity. Many human interactions take place on this plane, influencing thought processes. The spiritual plane deals with higher and more important visions and perceptions and universal oneness. It is not as easily accessible as the other two planes. The seven layers of the human energy field are clearly defined and have specific functions:

1. **Etheric/Vital Energy Body:** Existing on the physical plane, this body is said to be located up to 2 inches from the human body. It is a provider of health, life, and vitality, maintaining the body's yin/yang balance. Its consciousness is expressed in terms of physical sensations such as pleasure or pain.

2. **Emotional Energy Body:** Extending 1–3 inches from the physical body, this body's consciousness is expressed in terms of personal emotions, such as love, fear, and hatred. It is the field through which the emotional energy flows.

3. **Mental Energy Body:** This is a structured body extending 3–8 inches from the physical body. Its consciousness is expressed in terms of thinking that includes words, thoughts, and images.

4. **Astral Energy Body:** This is an amorphous body, extending 6–12 inches from the physical body. Existing on the astral/psychic etheric plane, it is a provider of imagination, desires, and psychic abilities. Dreams, hallucinations, fantasies, and visions are all astral experiences.

5. **Etheric Template Body:** Existing on the spiritual plane, it extends about 1½–2 feet from the physical body. It is expressed in terms of higher will—those who fail to get things done are believed to have a weak etheric template body.

6. **Celestial Energy Body:** Existing on the spiritual plane, it extends 2–2½ feet from the physical body. Associated with feelings of unconditional love and joy, this layer allows for the experience of spiritual ecstasy.

7. **Ketheric Template Body:** Extending about 2½–3½ feet from the physical body, this body is associated with knowledge of higher concepts and enables creative thoughts. Its consciousness can also be expressed in terms of a higher spiritual inspiration.

Dark Energy: The Unseen Force in the Universe

Dark energy is one of the most mysterious subjects of modern-day physics. It was first observed in 1998, and even though nearly two decades have passed since then, physicists throughout the world are still clueless about what dark energy is and how it affects everyone. Many theories explaining this relationship have been proposed. The discovery of the existence of dark energy has even fueled speculation that it could be linked to paranormal phenomena.

HOW WAS DARK ENERGY DISCOVERED?

For many years, physicists believed that the universe was expanding, but that it would eventually slow down because of the force of gravity between distant stars and galaxies. However, in 1998, observations made by the Hubble Space Telescope showed that the universe is in fact expanding at an accelerating pace. Not only was this completely unexpected, but scientists were unable to explain the reason behind it. Eventually, physicists came up with the explanation that a "dark energy" permeates the universe and that almost 70 percent of the universe consists of nothing but this energy.

NATURE OF DARK ENERGY

Very few facts are known about dark energy. It is believed that it has a uniform structure and remains essentially the same throughout the universe. It has an extremely low density, which makes it very hard to make any observations about it through conventional experiments.

The leading theory of dark energy is that it is an inherent property of space. Wherever there is space, there is a uniformly distributed dark energy in it. This theory comes from Einstein's theory of general relativity, which uses a "cosmological constant" to explain how the universe is held together. Many scientists now believe this cosmological constant is dark energy.

Another theory is that dark energy is a dynamic energy fluid called *quintessence*. Its name comes from the Greek concept of a pure "fifth element," or the *aether* that fills up the universe. Proponents of this theory believe that dark energy is not uniform and that it can change in time and space.

IS DARK ENERGY RELATED TO PARANORMAL PHENOMENA?

A lot of people now believe that the existence of dark energy is intricately linked to paranormal phenomena. Several theories explaining this relationship have been proposed in the last few years. Dark energy could:

- Explain how spirits can move objects and make them float in the air.
- Offer a reason why the conventional laws of physics do not apply to spirits.
- Act as the channel through which some people are able to communicate with spirits or through which telepathic communication can take place between two people.

THE MANY NAMES OF CONSCIOUSNESS

Dark energy can also help explain the concept of a universal consciousness (also known as distributed or nonlocal consciousness), which has been proved by several experiments. It could be the same phenomenon that has been referred to in various cultures as *chi, orgone, prana, aether,* or *the Holy Spirit.*

Other theories that relate paranormal phenomena to dark energy have been raised as well:

- Dark energy might carry psychic information and facilitate ghostly activity and psychic abilities.
- Dark energy might be able to pass through objects made of matter as if they do not exist.
- The spirit might be composed of dark energy that exists in symbiosis with matter of the human body when a person is alive. After a person's death, this energy is separated from the body.

Dark energy could in fact be the key that unlocks the relationship between science and paranormal phenomena, and the next few years could be very exciting for both these fields.

Parallel Universes and Multiple Existences

The idea of parallel universes stems from a key principle of quantum mechanics that everything has a probability associated with it, even reality as you know it. What's more, all possible outcomes are likely to exist at some point. In other words, one form of reality gradually slips into another form. To better understand this, consider the example of a die. When you throw the die, you may see it landing on one value, but quantum mechanics says that it lands on all values! This problem baffled physicists for a long time, until it was proposed that each outcome of throwing a die exists in a different universe and that a huge number of such parallel universes exist.

A COPY OF YOU SOMEWHERE OUT IN SPACE

In a parallel universe scenario, there are many copies of the same particles existing in multiple universes. By applying a quantum mechanics–based probabilistic framework, scientists argue that in such a scenario, different copies of the same person must also exist in multiple universes. These copies would be more or less identical, but there could be some key differences among them. In fact, different universes could even have different physical laws governing them.

IMPLICATIONS ON THE CONCEPT OF AFTERLIFE

In a parallel universe scenario, the concepts of life and afterlife take on entirely different meanings. There is no single "you" living in a single universe. There are many states of "you" living in universes next to each other.

When you take an action or when some other event takes place, there is a chance that, depending on the outcome of that event, different copies of you will branch out into different universes. Death is one such event. When we see someone dying, that reality may exist only in the universe that we are in. There may be a copy of that person that lives on in a different universe.

IS IT SCIENTIFICALLY POSSIBLE TO COMMUNICATE WITH SOMEONE IN A PARALLEL UNIVERSE?

It may seem that when a copy of you branches out into a different universe, it will be impossible for it to communicate with this universe. But physicists believe that interaction among different universes does take place. In fact, it has been proposed that this interaction is the cause behind one of the most fundamental forces of nature: gravity.

As far as we know, it is not possible for a copy of a person to come back into the same universe, but there could be ways through which he can send back messages for his loved ones. These messages would seem like paranormal activity to you, as they may not conform to the conventional laws of physics applicable to our universe. They could take the form of apparitions, unexplained voices, forces moving objects, etc. It is possible that psychics are also able to establish such communication through their ability to reach out to different universes.

Parallel universes and multiple existences used to be the fantasy of science-fiction writers. Today, with the research in string theory and quantum mechanics, these realms may indeed be possible. Present-day mathematical models are being developed in order to understand these possibilities in greater detail.

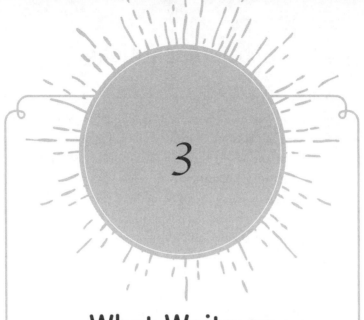

3

What Waits on the Other Side? Types of Spirits

You've probably heard myriad terms for beings from the other side—ghosts, demons, angels, spirits, poltergeists, and so on. But what do those terms actually mean? Read on to find out who might be communicating from the other side—and why.

Ghosts/Apparitions

The fear of ghosts and the supernatural is ingrained in every human being right from childhood. Some ghosts and apparitions have been revealed as fakes and illusions, but there are still many instances from different parts of the world that cannot be dismissed with rational explanations. A ghost or apparition is an actual physical form or manifestation of a formerly living being. Sometimes the ghost can actually interact with the environment and people present there. In some cases, the living may sense distinctive smells, sounds, or even voices, which can be associated with the long-dead person.

MESSAGES FROM THE OTHER SIDE

Battlefields where many fought and died are the perfect settings for residual hauntings. Many tourists to Gettysburg Battlefield in Pennsylvania have reported speaking with a man who was barefoot, dressed in ragged clothes, and wearing a floppy hat. The "man" disappeared after exchanging a few words.

Apparitions or ghosts are remnants of the life force of humans. It is generally believed that souls linger in our world as ghosts because they have "unfinished business." But there are many ghosts and apparitions that continue to stay on here because of a strong emotional bond with the living.

There are several different types of ghosts you could encounter, and crisis apparitions and poltergeists are some of the most common that have been discovered.

CRISIS APPARITIONS

Crisis apparitions often appear when the actual living person is undergoing the occurrence that will lead to his death. The most famous of these is the 1893 sighting of Vice-Admiral Sir George Tryon by guests at his wife's tea party back at home. The vice-admiral, dressed in official formals, walked through his home at the exact moment his ship sank with him off the coast of Syria.

POLTERGEISTS

A poltergeist is a manifestation of a restless soul in the form of telekinetic activity. The presence of such a ghost may result in moving objects, sounds, equipment malfunction, and other similar activity. It might begin as scratching noises from within the walls and escalate to more frequent banging or thumping sounds. Poltergeists are also known to create fires in different parts of the home or make words appear on surfaces.

MESSAGES FROM THE OTHER SIDE

One interesting and strangely touching poltergeist story is the report of Danny, aged seven, who wouldn't let anyone sleep in the bed that his mother died in nearly 100 years earlier. The case came into the spotlight in the late 1990s when another family bought the antique bed. The poltergeist not only wrote down its name and age but also categorically warned the family with a written message saying, "No one sleep in bed."

There is often a teenager in the house where the manifestations occur, but it is also possible for adults to trigger the manifestations. Often these cases involve a person who is troubled emotionally. Although largely unexplained, psychokinetic energy has been demonstrated to exist. Usually, people have no idea they are causing the poltergeist activity, which is happening all around them, and they are surprised to find that there is any possibility they themselves could be making the chaotic events happen.

MESSAGES FROM THE OTHER SIDE

To be fair, not all cases of poltergeist activity involve troubled individuals. The three most famous cases of poltergeist activity in the United States are:

- The Amityville haunting, which became the basis for both a book and a movie. (*The Amityville Horror* is generally considered to have been blown out of proportion for the sake of a story.)
- The case upon which author William Peter Blatty based *The Exorcist*
- The nineteenth-century Bell Witch case

All three hauntings have ended up as movies, with many dramatic additions to the story. *The Exorcist* is the best known of these three, and perhaps one of the most interesting aspects of this story is that Blatty based his book on a diary kept by a priest who assisted at the exorcism. He changed the lead character from a fourteen-year-old boy to a twelve-year-old girl. He has stated that 80 percent of what appears in the book is fact according to the priest.

The typical poltergeist disturbance does not last long. Disturbances usually subside after just a few weeks, although there are reports of some lasting years. The common conceptual framework is that elemental spirits are believed to comprise what the ancients perceived as the building blocks of the world—earth, air, fire, and water. Elementals are often described as primitive and malevolent beings or forces that attach themselves to a particular location.

Magicians and sorcerers believed they could use these spirits to do their bidding through a process called binding, which protected the person doing the spell from harm and allowed her to control the spirit as it did whatever task she assigned it. Sometimes this can backfire, a fact to which many dabblers in the occult can attest.

MESSAGES FROM THE OTHER SIDE

One famous story of the elemental takes place at Leap Castle in Ireland. Leap has a long and bloody history of strife, discord, and murder. The local people have always believed it to be haunted. In the late nineteenth century, an English couple, Jonathan and Mildred Darby, inherited Leap. Like so many other people at that time, Mildred Darby was interested in the occult. She held several séances at the castle with unwelcome results. When she began to dabble with the occult, she apparently awakened a terrifying elemental.

In the journal *Occult Review*, in 1909, Mildred described her experience with the creature she summoned: "I was standing in the Gallery looking down at the main floor, when I felt somebody put a hand on my shoulder. The thing was about the size of a sheep. Thin, gaunt, shadowy . . . its face was human, to be more accurate, inhuman. Its lust in its eyes, which seemed half decomposed in black cavities, stared into mine. The horrible smell one hundred times intensified came up into my face, giving me a deadly nausea. It was the smell of a decomposing corpse."

Hauntings

Contrary to popular belief, hauntings are more common than ghosts. A haunting is a "replay" of a happening that occurred years ago. Certain shocking or horrific incidents can affect the location where they took place so significantly that the incident is repeated as if it were a ghostly movie. Specific circumstances trigger this "movie," or it may just happen unexpectedly. Some researchers theorize that it may be some kind of specific point in time, caught in a repeating loop, over and over.

RESIDUAL HAUNTINGS

If the same apparition is seen over and over again, doing exactly the same thing, if the same sounds are heard at the same time of day, or if the same scene plays out over and over again over a period of years or even centuries, it is a residual haunting. Also called energy remnants or a memory imprint, the apparition in a residual haunting never interacts with onlookers, but rather seems totally oblivious to them.

Perhaps residual hauntings are simply playbacks of past events. The apparitions involved may not even be actual spirits but just impressions or recordings of events that were so traumatic that they have become imprinted on the very materials of the space in which they occurred.

There are many theories regarding residual hauntings. One of the first to offer a possible hypothesis of how residual hauntings occur was Thomas Charles Lethbridge, in his 1961 book *Ghost and Ghoul*. His theory is that just as audiotapes and videotapes record sounds and images, certain materials used in the construction of older structures may record impressions of events. If a traumatic, emotionally charged incident occurs, these materials record it for future playback. The event can suddenly occur and play out without an apparent cause. Sometimes there is no visual component to it, only repetitive sounds, such as footsteps, breathing, or smells that have no apparent cause. No one knows what triggers the playback of these recordings. It could be anything from the observer's own emotional state or sensitivity to weather conditions, such as high humidity or barometric pressure. Whatever its cause, the residual haunting is intriguing.

MESSAGES FROM THE OTHER SIDE

Older structures often have quartz, iron, and slate in them, and these materials are thought to hold impressions of the events in cases of residual hauntings. Europe has many ancient structures made of porous stones, which might function like batteries to store energy. This could explain why there are so many haunted sites in Europe. New England, as one of the oldest settled regions in the country, seems to be particularly prone to hauntings as well.

INTELLIGENT HUMAN HAUNTINGS

Incidents involving ghosts that have not yet crossed over, have unfinished business, or are too emotionally attached to a person or place and can't move on are classified as intelligent human hauntings. They linger for a reason. They are trying to get your attention. These entities can interact with humans and sometimes do so in a spectacular fashion.

Look for these signs of an intelligent haunting:

- Objects that disappear and then reappear in impossible places
- Cold spots and the strong sense of a presence or someone watching
- Strange, unexplained sounds

- Furniture and small objects being moved—sometimes even thrown
- Doors and windows opening and closing
- Lights, televisions, radios, and faucets turning on and off on their own

These apparitions have a mission to complete and they are looking for assistance—possibly your assistance. If the ghost is interactive and trying to communicate, it is most definitely an intelligent human haunting.

Sometimes this sort of haunting occurs shortly after a friend or loved one dies. It is as if he is trying to comfort or communicate with those left behind.

EMOTIONS AND SPIRITUAL PRESENCE ARE CONNECTED

The highest concentrations of paranormal activity can be found where there has been a great deal of human suffering and pain, trauma, or a strong emotion, such as fear or desperation. Surprisingly, cemeteries aren't that high on the list, but prisons, sanitariums, and hospitals are.

Intelligent hauntings without a human component have been documented. Animals that become attached to a location or person can also be interactive and thus termed intelligent hauntings. This is particularly true of pets, such as cats and dogs.

In intelligent hauntings, the entity retains the personality and appearance of the deceased person or animal. Sometimes, it may even appear wearing the same clothing it was wearing before passing over.

When an entity is strongly attached to a specific site, person, or object, it may try to protect it. This is a common occurrence. After all, when a person dies, he may not even realize it. If he has lived in a house for years, he may refuse to leave it even after he has passed on. He may think the new residents are trespassers and may naturally try to scare them into leaving.

Demons: Dangerous Entities

The American Heritage Dictionary, Fifth Edition, defines a demon as:

1. An evil supernatural being; a devil.
2. A persistently tormenting person, force, or passion: *the demon of drug addiction*.
3. One who is extremely zealous, skillful, or diligent: *worked away like a demon; a real demon at math*.
4. Variant of *daimon*.

This entity is quite distinct from both a ghost and an apparition. A demon is characterized by the added component of evil—it's a being that takes delight in tormenting the living. It implies a malicious and active type of haunting, which is quite different from a residual haunting, which is like a recorded version of an event that plays and replays over decades or even centuries. The entities in a residual haunting do not seem to be aware of onlookers and don't interact with them in any way.

Demonics, on the other hand, seem to want to interact; indeed, they seem to derive a lot of pleasure from doing so. Reports of these creatures predate the Bible, and accounts of them have existed in one form or another in every civilization of which we have a record. They were often simply called evil spirits. The word *demon* is derived from the Greek *daimon*, and in ancient Iran and India they were called *daewon*. These malevolent spirits were perceived in the Christian tradition as fallen angels. Whatever you call them, they are bad news. Dealing with these spirits requires preparation, an abundance of caution, and most definitely some outside help.

Ectoplasmic Mists and Fogs

The term *ectoplasm* came into use in 1894, when French physiologist Charles Richet coined the term to describe the misty substance associated with the formation of ghosts and believed to be the actual physical substance created by the energy manifested by mediums. Richet, winner of the Nobel Prize in Physiology or Medicine in 1913, was also the first to use the word *metaphysics* to describe what previously had been called *materialization*.

This rubbery, milky substance could appear either as a solid or a vapor. Extruded from the body of the medium, it would subsequently materialize limbs, faces, and even entire bodies. These manifestations were reportedly warm, flexible, and even doughlike. They emerged from orifices such as the mouth, ears, nose, and, occasionally, less convenient locations.

PROPERTIES OF ECTOPLASM

Forms of ectoplasm vary widely—anything from mists to thin tentacles or full bodies. This substance disappears when exposed to light and snaps back quickly into the medium's body. It was once believed that touching the ectoplasm or exposing it to light might cause injury to the medium. This was one of the main reasons mediums insisted that séances take place in almost total darkness, as it was believed that any attempt to touch or approach the mediums or ectoplasm could cause severe bodily harm. Daniel Dunglas Home was one notable exception to this rule; he conducted séances and manifested spirits in full daylight in the 1880s. The fact that these ectoplasmic manifestations occurred in semidarkness and that some were obvious frauds has cast a negative pall over the whole issue. Of the hundreds of shots of ectoplasm in existence, about 95 percent are less than convincing.

WHAT ARE ORBS?

Some investigators insist that orbs are nothing more than a side effect of a camera flash going off too close to the lens and bouncing off dust, bugs, or other particles in the air, such as raindrops. Others counter that they can indeed be evidence of paranormal activity or even entities themselves.

IMAGES OF MISTS AND LIGHTS

In metaphysical photography, shots that show fogs, mists, and odd-looking lights are often intriguing. In these cloudy shots, it is nearly impossible to tell what the vapor and mists represent.

Perhaps some can be dismissed as ordinary light pollution, reflections, or cigarette smoke, but when all these things have been eliminated, there still remain an impressive number of cloudy images and foggy forms caught by photographers.

MESSAGES FROM THE OTHER SIDE

Founded in 1884, the Berkeley Memorial Chapel, now St. Columba's Chapel in Middletown, Rhode Island, is one of the most beautiful stone chapels in New England. It looks as if it has been transported by magic from the English countryside to nestle among the old beeches in the churchyard. In a photograph taken of the church, the chapel appears to be filled with a swirling mist, although the mist wasn't apparent to the photographer when the shot was taken. The gravestones and memorials in the churchyard also appear to have streamers of smoke or fog trailing off them.

One of the most striking examples of misty figures appears in a You-Tube video entitled "Gettysburg Ghost -- Most Authentic video to date? Location 2," where several misty figures can be seen emerging from the tree to the left of the screen at the 1:55 mark. Check it out for yourself at www.youtube.com/watch?v=G39FMA26NK8, and prepare to be amazed. Of course, once you read the comments beneath the video you may start to doubt—which is good. You should always doubt, then examine the evidence.

Angels: Messengers and Guides

The word *angel* was derived from the Greek word *angelos*, which means "messenger." Angels have played a pivotal role in many world religions, perhaps most acutely in the context of Christianity. Angels were primarily the emissaries of God, providing people mentioned in the Bible with due and proper instruction as to what God intended for them. Sometimes their role extended beyond mere mouthpieces for the heavenly master; they were avenging creatures sent to punish and destroy the wicked.

MESSENGERS FIRST

Saint Augustine, the early Christian theologian and philosopher, aptly described angels: "Angels are spirits, but it is not because they are spirits that they are angels. They become angels when they are sent. For the name angel refers to their office, not their nature. You ask the name of this nature, it is spirit; you ask its office, it is that of an Angel, which is a messenger."

Millions around the world believe in angels. From every culture and geographic location and period in history, we have heard about angels. Angels are known as spiritual beings, messengers of God, or spirits of the dead transformed after passing that are historically described as God's task force, protectors, and guides for people in the earthly realm. They are often portrayed in art, literature, and other media as winged beings, filled and shrouded with light, often androgynous looking, sometimes with halos, and dressed in white, resplendent with the qualities of love, kindness, protection, joy, glory, destiny, healing, justice, protection, and celestial power.

THE ARCHANGELS

In Christian tradition, there are seven archangels: Gabriel, Raphael, Michael, Uriel, Jophiel, Zadkiel, and Samuel (sometimes spelled Chamuel). Lucifer was the eighth archangel. He was cast out of heaven and became the leader of the dark angels, or demons.

ANGELS IN MAJOR RELIGIONS

Angels have something of an irrational portrayal, with some cultures and belief systems hailing them as the absolute embodiment of purity and mercy, and others as terrifying creatures of righteous wrath.

A common theme noted within all religions is that angels are prohibited from acting directly in human affairs, whether by active choice or merely a design quirk. This means that they cannot make decisions for you or take control of your life.

Angels in Christianity

Two angels were sent to redeem and spy on Sodom and Gomorrah, cities of ill repute, according to the Bible. When the angels were sexually assaulted, God decided that the cities were to be destroyed, despite the angels' pleas for clemency.

The archangel Michael is given an especially important and pivotal role in the Bible, and his cameo appearance is specifically mentioned in the Book of Revelation, which heralds and discusses the "end of days" in great detail. Michael, it is claimed, will defeat the "great dragon" (Satan) and then seal him in hell for all of eternity in order to usher in an eternal calm.

Angels in Buddhism

Despite its general rejection of an afterlife, Buddhism does make provision for the existence of angels. Unlike Christian angels, angels in Buddhism (commonly referred to as *devas*) come into being when pure-hearted people reach a sufficiently high level of enlightenment, which allows them to reach a higher spiritual plane. However, just like their Christian counterparts, they are not supposed to directly meddle in the affairs of men; to do so is a divine offense. They do act as custodians of moral conduct, rewarding those who are virtuous and kind, and harassing those who are wicked and selfish.

Angels in Islam

A belief in angels is a mandatory prerequisite for a true Muslim. Indeed, a rejection of the existence of these celestial beings will render that person the status of non-*mu'min*, or nonbeliever.

ANGEL INTERVENTIONS

According to angelologists, the intervention of angels in human lives is not limited to our physical death. Angels guide souls to the divine light and love of God and help them reach their ultimate destination. And while people are in this world, angels provide healing, love, guidance, and protection whenever a person calls upon them and seeks their help. Guardian angels are spiritual beings, and each person has at least one angel watching. They are present during an individual's graduation ceremony, a birthday party, or other happy occasions that mark a turning point in life, to guide that person toward the right path. And when people face emergencies, such as a life-threatening situation, angels can help them avoid all dangers and keep them safe if it is meant to be.

MESSAGES FROM THE OTHER SIDE

People have reported hearing voices in their heads that have guided them toward incredible achievements that normally would not have been possible. Some people talk about how a stranger or loved one suddenly arrived and saved them in a life-threatening situation. There are numerous instances where everyday people have reported encounters with angels. Encounters can happen through a light or a distinct voice, or an angel might appear in human form—as a friend, relative, or stranger—to assist a person in his time of need.

As Doreen Virtue writes in her article "Calling All Angels," you can connect with angels and ask for help by writing a letter spelling out your need, visualizing them, or just calling out aloud and asking for their guidance and assistance.

Angels can act as messengers and guides only when a person is prepared to listen to them. Intuition can help people hear the signs and messages given by angels, since they are always working to protect humans against unpleasant events and to help them achieve life's real purpose.

Life-Saving Interventions

Angels often intervene to prevent accidents and death. In an account from firefighter Mark Kuck, retold in *The Big Book of Angels*, an angelic voice gave warning and instruction to the firefighter, allowing him to save his life and the life of his partner. While fighting a fire in a mobile home, Kuck heard a clear male voice:

> "Mark," it said, "you need to go." Mark was astonished. The voice was audible, yet it couldn't be his partner—he was too far away to be heard. And an air pack distorts a voice. . . . Not like this voice, so distinct and close it was almost at his ear. Nor were there any openings in the trailer where someone outside could yell through. What was happening?
>
> After Kuck and his partner retreated, the flames advanced into the room they had been in. If they had not left at the moment Kuck heard the voice, they would have perished. Later, as the fire waned, Mark thought more seriously about the voice. It had been a young voice, something like his own, firm but not intimidating, a voice that he instinctively knew he could trust and obey. And, yes, he had heard it once before, when he was seventeen and involved in a serious automobile accident. Wasn't it this same voice that had calmed him as he crashed, reassured him that all would be well? But how could this be?

In another account from bush pilot Terry Baldwin, retold by Daniel J. Benor in *Personal Spirituality*, we again find a human-sounding voice said to be an angel intervening. Baldwin was flying passengers through the bush when they were caught in a dangerous storm, and his instruments began to fail. An apparent air traffic controller led them to safety through the storm, evidently using only radar instructions, as the passengers prayed openly. However, Baldwin lost touch with the voice when the radio broke off, and another voice appeared suddenly, just as the plane touched down to safety. At this point, Baldwin said:

> "Thanks, tower. There's little doubt that you saved our lives today." The controller's reply cast a stunned silence over the men in the plane.
> "What are you talking about? We lost contact with you about forty miles out."

MESSAGES FROM THE OTHER SIDE

There have been many famous stories of angel interventions in the lives of artists and historical figures alike, guiding their acts and works, from Joan of Arc to Handel to William Blake. Contemporary research and literature have documented accounts of angel interventions that involve visions, audible information, smells, and tactile sensations. Angels are also often reported to appear as similar to regular human beings, as stated by Daniel J. Benor in *Personal Spirituality: Science, Spirit, and the Eternal Soul*. Benor claims that many angels are "described as looking like normal people who appear out of nowhere, give their assistance, and then disappear again into nowhere. They may communicate in gestures, words or telepathically."

In this case, as in many other accounts, prayers often come directly before an angel intervention.

According to Carmel Reilly in *True Tales of Angel Encounters*, aside from miraculous life-saving encounters, we often hear of angel interventions where angels appear as guardian angels in everyday experiences, in dreams, or during meditation or prayer. There are also stories of angels sharing messages or news, performing real physical acts, and acting as spirit guides and ghosts.

Angels and Near-Death Experiences

There are also many recounted instances of angels being present in near-death experiences as well as out-of-body experiences. As professor Craig R. Lundahl stipulates in an article entitled "Angels in Near-Death Experiences," "Angels are personages with whom the NDEr [near-death experiencer] does not usually recall having previous acquaintance. Angels serve as guides, messengers, or escorts in the NDE." Lundahl writes that in one account of a near-death experience, "a man . . . came close to dying as a result of being ill during a tooth extraction, and took a trip to heaven where he saw angels." In another account, there was a woman "who described angels holding hands to form a stairway to heaven."

CHILDREN AND ANGELS

Children often tell compelling stories in which they encounter angels. According to Carmel Reilly in *True Tales of Angel Encounters*, there are "a large number of reports of guardian angels helping children who were ill or lost that were quite similar," as well as many other situations in which a child was in distress.

Reilly explains that many researchers theorize that children are often the recipients of angel interventions because they are more "vulnerable" and "less rigid" than adults, and are more open to contact with the unknown and the divine.

GUARDIAN ANGELS AND YOU

As you can see from this discussion about angels, many of them are guardian angels. A guardian is defined as someone who takes charge or care of someone else. A guardian angel is considered to be a spirit being that watches over a human. Your own angelic or spirit guides may be people you already know. It is possible that a friend or relative who is now on the other side could act as a guide for you in this lifetime and look out for you.

ASK FOR HELP

If you are having trouble defining who is watching over you from the other side, you may want to go for a psychic reading. A competent and ethical psychic may have the ability to recognize who is watching out for and working with you.

Do you believe you have a guardian angel or angels who watch over you? Have you ever seen your angels? If so, what do they look like? Can you hear your angels speaking to you? If so, what are they saying? How often and under what circumstances do your angels visit you—daily, weekly, or only occasionally?

Can you feel your angels around you? If so, when do you feel them? Have your angels produced certain smells or tastes for you to experience? Have you ever heard their wings or other sounds that let you know they are with you?

You do not need to see an angel to recognize that one is there with you. Validation can happen in many ways. Keeping a record of your miracles also reminds you that your team of angels is at work, whether you see them or not. If you feel that you have angels watching over you, then give them credit for the good job they are doing.

Once you accept that there is a good possibility of a guide or guides connected to you, you can begin to develop confidence that there really is someone there to help you handle both minor and major problems.

You can actually have a conversation with your guides, even though it may seem to be a one-way conversation. Just believing that someone hears you can give you confidence that you are not alone.

The other side may not appear to you while you are in a waking state. Many times your guides will visit you in your dream state. This is especially true if you have an active conscious mind that is constantly cluttered with your thoughts. Your psychic communication often comes into your awareness when your active mind stops to rest. The only time you relax may be when you sleep.

Other Types of Spirits Out There

In addition to angels and the souls of those who have passed on to the other side, there are other nonphysical entities that exist in the spirit world. A spirit may be a fairy, power animal, or another entity. Some people believe that spirits are evil and fear that communicating with a spirit is working with the devil. Others are afraid that communicating with spirits will lead to losing control of their body, mind, and spirit.

EXORCISMS

An exorcism is a rite that is performed by a priest of the Catholic Church to rid a victim of the evil spirit or spirits that possess him. Other religions perform their own types of exorcisms. For example, Pentecostal Christians use the laying-on of hands.

The fear of spirit possession is very real to many people. Making sure to surround yourself with a protective bubble of unconditionally loving energy can help you on your journey of psychic development. At the same time, if you encounter a strong negative force for any reason, stop what you are doing and seek the advice of a professional psychologist or clergy member who has a background in working with spirit possession.

On the other hand, you may consider a spirit to be something that can be your guide and help you through life. You may have an image in your mind of what a spirit looks like. You may already be working with a spirit. A spirit that is there to help you is called a spirit guide.

Spirits can have particular shapes and roles, such as:

- **Fairies:** These are spirits that resemble tiny people. Fairies live in the woods and are known for their magical powers. They are a part of Celtic lore and are especially popular with children, probably due to their small size.

- **Gatekeepers:** In the psychic world, these are spirit guards that watch out for you as you travel about in other realms. A gatekeeper is your strong and powerful guide and protector. You can count on this being to help keep your energy centers in balance and control what enters and leaves.

- **Power animals:** Animals have been connected to mysticism since time immemorial. If you have a power animal, it could be one from nature, such as a wolf or a bear. It could be a domestic pet, perhaps one that crossed over but still lingers with you to watch over and comfort you.

Whatever your spirits are, they may visit you in your dreams. Do you have dreams that include forms of spirit guides or animals? If so, how often do you dream about them? Do they come for specific reasons that relate to your life situation at that time? Do they have messages for you from beyond?

PART 2

Communicating with the Other Side

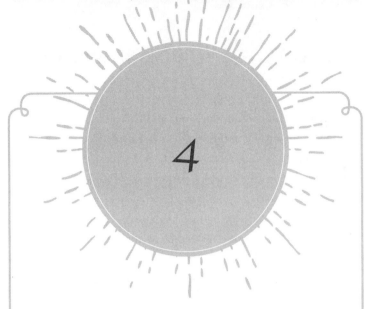

Tuning In to Your Psychic Abilities

Did you know that you are psychic? You are, even though you may not think so. Many people do not understand this special natural ability. It is often unwelcome and misunderstood, not only by psychics but also by family, friends, and strangers. This chapter will provide you with an introduction to the psychic world and what it means to be psychic. You will learn about the levels of consciousness, psychic intuition, and how to enter a state of focus. You'll also learn how to connect to your third eye, a location in the body through which many psychics receive their information.

Discovering What Is Inside You

Everyone is psychic. Everything that you have experienced so far in this lifetime has helped develop your ability. Your psychic ability, like any other talent or characteristic, is a product of your physical self, your environment, your relationships, and your inherited genetics. Remember that you are the keeper of your own ability. It is there waiting to be put to positive use. No matter what you read or what others tell you, it is your soul that knows the answers. The goal here is for you to identify and become comfortable with your own special psychic abilities.

Unfortunately, the idea of being psychic often conjures up the image of gypsy fortunetellers or pay-per-minute phone psychics. And like in any industry, there are some bad apples out there who only want to fleece you out of your hard-earned money with their "mystical insights." Nowadays, certain books and programs focus on helping you control the world around you for your sole benefit. As a result, many people try to misuse their gifts for self-gain rather than to benefit the universe and help others along the pathways of life.

Because it is different for every person, it is impossible to explain exactly what the psychic process is like. No one else has a mind that is identical to yours. Many psychic courses designed to enhance intuitive abilities are taught using a model that the instructor prefers. However if you, the participant, are not of a similar mind, your initial enthusiasm can easily turn to frustration.

Try to think of it like this: Each soul has a map to follow during its lifetime. The map should be used as a guide to learning life lessons and resolving old karma. Whether or not you follow this map is your individual choice. You must use your free will to choose to become in tune with your psychic ability.

Opening Yourself to Communication

The question of whether life continues in some form after death is still being debated, without any widely accepted answer as of yet. Messages from the dead, communication through symbols, visitations by the dead in dreams, and many other occurrences point to some channel of communication existing between our world and that of the spirits—a channel that you could tap into. If you desire to make connections to the afterlife, the key is to remain open to all possibilities of communication.

WHY WOULD YOU WANT TO COMMUNICATE?

The purpose of afterlife communication differs from person to person. Those left behind often try to reach out to the dead to assuage their grief or any guilt associated with the person's death. Being able to talk to or sense the dead person can bring you a feeling of closure and may ease the pain of the loss. Many turn to their dead relatives for guidance or advice during difficult times. A Ouija board or similar communication tool may be used, or a medium may act as a link to the deceased.

In many other instances, it is the spirit that initiates communication. The spirit may wish to complete unfinished business or help family members during troubled times. (A well-publicized occurrence was the appearance of farmer James Chaffin's spirit to disclose the whereabouts of his will to his son.) Other spirits simply want their family to know that they are happy. Symbolic or subliminal messages that can readily be associated with the deceased are often received in such cases. The deceased may also visit the living in their dreams.

KEEP AN OPEN MIND

Everybody loses a loved one at some point in their life. But only a few experience a sense of the deceased's continuing presence after the person's death. Mediums are able to sense these "people" due to their heightened perceptions or extraordinary talents (you'll read more about mediums in the next chapter). But many "normal" people with no special abilities have had similar experiences too. Researchers believe that to establish communication with the spirits, you must be prepared to believe when confronted with signs or symbols.

ACTIVELY PREPARING FOR SPIRIT COMMUNICATION

Before you contact a professional medium, you can try to establish a connection with the spirit yourself. This serves three purposes:

1. You can commit to your belief that you can communicate and this helps you keep an open mind about the process.

2. You are just as likely to sense your loved one's presence as a medium, who is a stranger.

3. You can "broadcast" your intent and hope to reach the deceased's spirit; this draws the spirit to communicating with you.

It is believed that spirits are in a different realm than the living because they are not burdened by flesh or mired in the complexities of our world. Electromagnetic instruments and other tools have been used to determine the variations in energetic vibrational frequencies between the dead and living (you'll learn more about those tools in Chapter 7). These variations make it difficult for the living to communicate easily with the dead. This is why mediums who can duplicate the vibration are able to reach a spirit at times when a loved one cannot.

There are many ways to become more receptive to sensing the presence of the dead:

○ **Cultivate a calm state of mind:** Anger, grief, guilt, fear, and other strong emotions are barriers to communication. They close your mind to the subtle signs and subliminal messages that may be conveyed by the spirits. Relax your mind and calm yourself before you try to "reach" your deceased loved ones.

○ **Create an open atmosphere:** The atmosphere of the area where you are initiating the communication must be calm and silent. Surround yourself with items associated with the deceased, like photographs, personal items, and other things that evoke positive memories of the person. These positive energies call to the spirit and also help keep negative energies at bay.

- **Consciously reach out to the spirit:** Make a conscious effort in your mind to reach out to the spirit. This, again, "broadcasts" your intent and need to communicate, and this need will draw the spirit to you.

- **Encourage a receptive dream state:** Just before you go to sleep, ask your loved one to contact you. Spirits find it the easiest to make contact through the dream state and will often meet you there to communicate. Keep a pad of paper and a pen or an audio recorder next to your bed so when you wake you can record any instances of contact that might have occurred.

COMMUNICATE WITH GOOD INTENTIONS

It is important that you ask for communication with the "highest and best intentions" and for it to be "surrounded with the white light of love." This will set the conditions of any contact and will filter out any unwanted residual energy in your field.

Be aware that it may take time; several attempts may be required to establish the link. The afterlife is still mostly shrouded in mystery. How the communication happens and what restrictions there are on the spirits are unknown, and every spirit may not be able to communicate in the same manner and at a time of its choosing. Sometimes you may get indirect answers or messages that are not relevant to your questions at all. Still, any such contact demonstrates the possibility of opening a channel of communication, and is a successful attempt.

A Basic Type of Communication: Thought and Prayer

Prayer is a means of establishing an emotional and spiritual connection with powers beyond our imagination and direct reach. Different people follow different praying methods and expressions of devotion. The object of this kind of devotion, affection, or faith can be a divinity, a person, a departed relative, an idea, or even a group with influential teachings and principles.

Different schools of belief may have different prescribed methods of prayer. These methods can take the form of hymns, songs, words, or various acts. Some people even choose to simply express their faith in their own words extemporaneously.

Most often, people turn to prayer seeking guidance during difficult times. Sickness or trouble of some kind can also prompt fervent prayers for help from the unseen. Deeply religious people believe that their daily prayers reveal to them the right path in life. The reasons for praying are different among different people, but the commitment, faith, and emotions behind the supplications are equally strong.

Praying allows the living to communicate with the universal powers and seek help from them beyond human means. The help desired may be material, spiritual, or emotional. Usually, humans faced with daily challenges of ill health, financial want, or emotional disturbances ask for material or emotional help, like release from a specific worry or anxiety.

THE EFFICACY OF PRAYERS

Skeptics question the efficacy of prayer in granting the devotee what he desires. But the fact is that devotees through the ages have, without doubt, gained emotional strength and risen above their worldly problems through the power of prayer. A prayer expressed with complete faith in a supreme power gives an immediate sense of calm to the devotee. A deep belief that you have the support and blessing of the power you believe in blossoms in your heart as a result of prayer, helping you face tribulations with confidence. Many medical studies have focused on the power of prayer in recent years, with results showing a significant difference in the healing of ill patients who engaged in prayer.

MESSAGES FROM THE OTHER SIDE

The effectiveness of prayer is perhaps most clearly illustrated by faith healings. The healing of many sick people by Jesus is recorded in the New Testament, establishing the way for many religious leaders to follow suit in later years. There are six incidents described in the four Gospels wherein Jesus restored sight to the blind. Greek mythology also speaks of the centaur Chiron, who could heal with his touch. Every religion has its own share of healing stories.

SEEKING HELP FROM BEYOND THE VEIL

Prayers can also take the form of supplications to loved ones who have passed beyond the veil, or transitioned to the other side. Often when a family member dies, the grieving survivors are unable to bear the loss. Praying to this departed soul can help bring closure to the grieving person and also help the restless spirit of the dead move on to the higher regions.

Most religions propagate the belief that upon death, the soul moves closer to God. Seeking help from such souls by means of prayer is a way to channel the infinite power of the Almighty to fulfill our desires. The need may not always be physical in nature, like money or a job. The supplicant can ask for peace, the ability to pray better, or the well-being of himself or others.

Many religions set aside a special day for communion with the dead. On this day, the dead are remembered by offering special gifts, food, and other items that they were particularly fond of in their lifetime. The Day of the Dead and All Saints' Day are examples of such celebrations when the dead are believed to be closest to the living and can actually partake of the offerings made by their living family members. The concept that the living are separated from the departed souls by an invisible "curtain" is an integral part of these religious traditions.

Praying is a very effective tool to channel the infinite powers that lie beyond our worldly reach. The old saying that "faith can move mountains" may not be taken literally in today's world, but it is something that should be seriously pondered. It signifies that deep devotion and heartfelt belief that entities beyond imagination and this world can help resolve human difficulties.

Your Psychic Intuition

Beyond thoughts and prayers lies another level of communication with the other side—your psychic abilities. When exploring your psychic abilities, it's helpful to start by thinking of your existence as a whole. You exist almost simultaneously in three different minds:

1. The **conscious mind** is your thinking mind and is aware of the events taking place around you.
2. Your **unconscious mind** is the place where all of your memories are stored. It is constantly sending images up to your conscious mind.
3. Your unconscious mind connects you to your third mind, the **Universal Mind**, which is the source of all knowledge in the universe, including the present, the past, and the future.

There are three types of psychic intuition:

1. **Deductive:** comes from the unconscious mind
2. **Random:** comes from the Universal Mind
3. **Goal-focused:** works through all three minds

Your mental makeup determines the type of intuition that is yours. Each person has a unique form of intuition that may be a blend of any of the three types.

DEDUCTIVE PSYCHIC INTUITION

Deductive psychic images come from your unconscious mind's ability to take in external sensory stimuli. That's not as complicated as it sounds. Your five sensory receivers—eyes, ears, mouth, skin, and nose—are constantly bombarded with stimuli in the form of external pictures, sounds, tastes, tactile sensations, temperature changes, and smells. You also experience external emotions or energies unrecognized by your conscious mind. You take in a lot of information that you are not consciously aware of because it is absorbed by the unconscious mind, where it is stored.

When your conscious mind has a question that it cannot answer, this question will also go to the unconscious mind, which will mull over the problem and rely on its stored data to come up with a response. In the meantime, your conscious mind usually goes on to another subject and forgets what it was looking for. But your unconscious mind stays hard at work. All of a sudden, out of nowhere, a psychic insight appears. Your unconscious mind has come to a logical psychic solution to your problem, one that your conscious mind hadn't thought of.

RANDOM PSYCHIC INTUITION

Random psychic intuition is different from deductive psychic intuition in several ways. It comes from your Universal Mind and may be totally unrelated to anything known or connected consciously or unconsciously to the psychic image. It could be about something that has taken place, is taking place, or will take place anywhere in the world. In other words, random psychic intuition can occur in any of the three phases of time—past, present, or future.

A random psychic experience often comes at a time when it is unexpected or even unwanted. It can be very powerful and leave you dazed and confused. This disorientation may last only a few moments, but its effects are powerful enough to last a lifetime. The experience itself may continue to live on in your mind long after the image first appeared.

Not all random psychic experiences are negative. It is possible that you might have a pleasant premonition; then later, you might realize that what you saw as nothing more than a happy daydream has become a reality. It may be that you suddenly get a set of numbers in your head that leads to a big jackpot win. Or a song may begin to play in your head that you haven't heard in years, a song that later you may unexpectedly hear on the radio or television.

Random psychic intuition happens when you are in a light trance state. It occurs when your conscious or critical mind is open to the images that are sent up from your unconscious and your Universal Mind. A random psychic trance can be triggered by external or internal stimuli. Once the intuitive trance process begins, it is hard to disengage from it until it has run its course.

GOAL-FOCUSED PSYCHIC INTUITION

Goal-focused psychic intuition is a combination of deductive and random intuition. Using this method, you can make a conscious effort to gain certain insights through psychic intuition. You can attempt to use your intuitive ability for a specific goal. Focused psychic intuition is the kind that is normally employed by professional psychics and others who already understand and use their intuitive abilities on a consistent basis.

Professional psychics who work with the police will often familiarize themselves with some of the facts of the case they are working on. Examining a piece of evidence or a photograph from a crime scene could provide intuitive information, and an actual visit to a specific location may also lead to new clues. Some of the information may be drawn from deductive intuition, and some may be generated at random, but all clues gathered are related to the specific goal of the psychic trance.

HOW DO FORTUNETELLERS WORK?

When you ask a fortuneteller to give you an answer about a specific problem in your life, the psychic will connect to her intuitive source and focus on the requested information. Then she will wait for her mind to download the information requested.

Entering a State of Focus

When your conscious mind's ability to think clearly is interrupted, you enter an altered state of focus. All people, whether they know it or not, go in and out of this state many times a day. When there, your critical reasoning is pushed aside. The power of suggestion, whether it's by your unconscious mind or by someone else, takes control of your thought process.

You can be guided or induced into a trance in several different ways. The trigger can come either through external stimuli—if, for instance, you were to enter a specific location—or through internal stimuli, such as thoughts or feelings. Trances can be positive or negative, and they can continue to influence you long after your initial experience. You can remain in a trance state for a few minutes or for days. The state will continue until something interrupts it. Once you recognize the trance state, you have the choice to remain in it or not.

MOVING THROUGH TIME

Your mind moves through three different phases of time: the past, the present, and the future. Everything that you have experienced in your lifetime—your past—is deposited in the memory bank of your unconscious mind. Sometimes the information is held there for years before it suddenly comes back up to the surface of your conscious mind. When you experience these memories again, you are actually focusing on a memory-induced altered state of consciousness. The stronger the memory, the stronger the focus.

HIGHWAY HYPNOSIS

Have you ever driven down the highway and become so absorbed in thought that you actually went right by your destination? You were in an altered state of focus when this occurred. Even though you were not totally aware of your location, you were still driving your vehicle safely. This phenomenon is called highway hypnosis.

It is also possible to focus on a future experience in the same way that you focus on a past experience. Some people see vivid images of events that have yet to happen. These images can come to the surface of your unconscious mind without warning when you are in a relaxed state or even while you are dreaming.

Your mind also experiences the present. In this time phase, your mind can distort speed and distance. Sometimes a minute seems like an hour, and sometimes an hour seems like a minute. In athletics, being in the present is called "being in the zone."

It is easy to get caught up in such an altered state of focus that you are unaware of what time phase you are in. This can be very confusing when it happens without warning. As you learn to balance the three phases of your mind and be aware of the past, future, and present altered states, it will be easier to understand how your mind focuses.

WHAT IS AN ALTERED STATE?

An altered state of consciousness occurs when a person is not necessarily aware of what he is experiencing. The conscious mind is not involved in making critical decisions. The person in a deep state may have no knowledge of external events.

PSYCHIC ALTERED STATES OF FOCUS

Psychic altered states of focus occur when your conscious mind is flooded with information that cannot be deduced by critical reasoning. Usually, this information comes from the unconscious and/or the Universal Mind, and it often comes at a time when you least expect it. Knowing what is going on within you is the key to being in tune with these altered states.

Everyone enters into one or more kinds of psychic altered states. Some have a great deal of meaning, while others seem to be there just to verify that you are capable of experiencing something unexplainable. Perhaps you have experienced knowing when the telephone was going to ring or thought of a song just before it played on the radio.

EXERCISE: CONTACT YOUR GUIDES

Take a deep breath, exhale, close your eyes, and begin to feel the connection through your crown chakra (on top of your head) down to your third-eye chakra (in the middle of your forehead). Allow yourself to feel the loving and peaceful energy of the universe as it flows downward into your body. Feel the unconditionally loving energy of the universe as it forms a protective bubble around your being. Feel the positive energy that keeps you in balance and leaves you free to be open to the universe's guides that have been assigned to you. Let yourself enjoy a brief moment of total freedom filled with peace and love.

RELEASE YOURSELF

Remember, you can always bring yourself out of an altered state of focus. All you have to do is take a deep breath, exhale, open your eyes, and come back to your conscious mind, feeling positive and safe.

Ask for permission to meet one or more of your guides in any positive form they may take. Allow yourself to relax, breathe in and out, and wait for a feeling of affirmation. This affirmation may come as a direct image, a voice, a pleasant sound, a feeling, or even a smell. You may experience nothing at first, so just wait patiently and believe that the right images will come to you. It is possible that this is not the right time to meet your guides.

You may get a faint image, or a lot of images swirling together. You may see colors, or you may hear a whole group of voices. If everything is going too fast, ask for help in slowing down your images. If you can, focus on just one image and concentrate on defining for yourself what you are sensing. Allow your guides to become comfortable in revealing themselves to you.

Many people have an idea of what their guides should be. You may or may not get the images you expected. Just being in the flow of positive peace and love is good for you. Just imagining your guides will bring you closer to them.

MAKE THE CONNECTION

If you are able to sense your guides, can you communicate with them? If so, which sense do you feel most comfortable using? Even if you see nothing, you may still ask questions. You may receive your answers in pictures, by voice or other sounds, by feelings that you can translate into words, or through positive and negative tastes and smells. You may have feelings in certain places in your body or some other sensation or image. You may ask if there is a name that you can call your guide(s).

The first step is to get an understanding of what you may be telling yourself through your guides. You may ask for guidance in many different aspects of your life, from health to your soul's purpose. Don't expect an answer right away. It might come then, or it might come in the near future. Always keep the feeling of universal peace and love flowing through you when you are making the connection to your guides. You may know that they are there, but you may never really see them. That's okay; the important thing is that they are with you.

Channeling Spirits

Another form of psychic communication and guidance is channeling. A channel is a conduit for something to pass through. A psychic channel is a person who has another entity or spirit communicate through her. This may be a voluntary or involuntary action on the part of the host body—the channel isn't always aware of what is taking place. Channeling can happen when you are in a trance or asleep.

When you act as a channel, your voice and mannerisms may change to reflect the personality of the entity that is coming through. During this time, the spirit may convey information through speech, automatic writing, or even different artistic forms. Many channels bring a message of peace from a higher source of knowledge.

EXPERIENCING CHANNELING

If you'd like to try your hand at channeling, it's a good idea to begin with someone experienced with the concept, like a hypnotherapist. She can help you enter a deep altered state of focus in a safe and positive environment.

You can also try automatic writing or typing by allowing yourself to enter a relaxed trance state, leaving your fingers free to be used by the spirit. Just ask that the right messages for that moment come through your hands and fingers. Like all other forms of psychic development, practice and patience will help your technique to improve.

Divination

Beyond using your intuition and channeling, there are other ways to communicate with those on the other side. Divination is a way of gathering information by paranormal means, using tools and symbols to acquire knowledge from the collective unconscious, the superconscious, or beings on a different plane of existence. This knowledge can be about people, places, or things from the past, present, or future.

The following are three major types of divination:

- **Necromancy** is a type of divination by means of communication with the dead.
- **Scrying** is foretelling the future using a crystal ball or other reflective object or surface.
- **Dowsing** is a means of locating different substances and energies through the use of two rods.

The tools of divination have their roots in antiquity. Since the dawn of time, humans have tried to contact and control the spirits of the dead. In this section, we'll discuss the types of divination used for that purpose, rather than those simply used to tell fortunes and predict future events, such as palmistry, card reading, or astrology.

NECROMANCY

The most famous tool of the necromancer is the Ouija board. The board as we know it dates back to the late nineteenth century. It was made popular during the spiritualist movement, when its widespread use was considered harmless. Today it has come into disfavor, as it is said to open a door to poltergeists and other low-level psychic phenomena. This door, once opened, is not easily shut, so many psychic investigators consider the Ouija board dangerous and seriously discourage its use.

The board's surface has the letters of the alphabet, the numerals 0 through 9, and the words *yes*, *no*, *hello*, and *goodbye*. A triangular device called a planchette, usually made of plastic and about 4 inches long, has enough room for two people to lightly rest their fingers on it. The planchette has three felt-tipped legs that glide over the board's surface, allowing it to point at letters, spelling out answers to questions asked by participants. In his article "Ouija: Not a Game," writer Dale Kaczmarek of the Ghost Research Society (GRS) warns that automatic writing and séances are dangerous for novice users.

Kaczmarek suggests that spirits from the lower astral plane are the entities most often attracted by these divination tools, and they introduce chaotic and sometimes even dangerous energy into the homes of the naive. Don't be tempted to use these devices without the proper safeguards and training. They have a long history of trouble.

SCRYING

Scrying is another form of divination, often used to foretell the future and communicate with the spirit world. Scrying was used by ancient cultures from Persia to Greece to Egypt as a tool for prognostication, or predicting future events. Spirits were thought to have a hand in conveying the messages. Nostradamus, arguably the most famous psychic of all time, is said to have used a small bowl of water as his means of seeing into the future. From the Middle Ages to present times, scrying has been widely used by wizards, witches, clairvoyants, and psychics.

Scryers most often use crystal balls or black mirrors, although any reflective media, even ink, water, and crystals, can be used. Most people are familiar with the image of the gypsy fortuneteller gazing raptly into a crystal ball to relate the fate of her gullible clientele.

The premise behind scrying is that when the person gazes into the reflective surface in the proper state of relaxation, she will see images that unfold either before her or in her mind's eye—glimpses of a future time, a far-off place, or a past event.

DOWSING

Dowsing is another form of divination used since ancient times to seek answers to questions. With this method, you can locate different substances and energies by using two rods, which cross when an energy field is encountered. The first recorded use of dowsing may be a cave painting at Tassili n'Ajjer in the Sahara, dated to approximately 6000 B.C.E. It shows a crowd gathered to watch a dowser at work. Ancient people frequently used dowsing rods to locate water.

Probably used initially to determine the will of the gods or find answers to questions about the future, dowsing is used widely today to locate things.

It has long been debated whether dowsing is possible due to an electromagnetic phenomena or an actual paranormal ability. Regardless, the process has withstood the test of time, despite its many detractors.

URI GELLER AND DOWSING

Sometimes pendulums of metal or crystal are used to dowse, particularly when the dowser is hoping to locate something on a map. Controversial psychic Uri Geller has stated on many occasions that the bulk of his income comes from dowsing to locate oil fields for the petroleum industry. In the 1970s, Geller underwent double-blind tests in which he was asked to locate a ball bearing, water, or a magnet concealed within identical metal containers. A third party placed the items in the containers, and scientists filmed Geller as tests were run repeatedly. Geller used a form of dowsing and correctly located the items in almost all of the tests. The scientists determined that the odds were a trillion to one that he had obtained his results by chance.

No one really knows how the dowsing process works. Is the subconscious moving the pendulum, or is a spirit or higher force doing it? Is it biofeedback and bioenergy? Theories and speculation continue.

Learning to Dowse

Perhaps the simplest way for beginners to learn to dowse is with a pendulum. You need a pendulum, metal bobber, or crystal and a chain or string to suspend it from. Make sure you're comfortable with the dowsing tool and are away from any noise, distractions, or electronic equipment.

1. Determine a system for yourself; for instance, clockwise may mean yes, counterclockwise no.
2. Relax by taking three or four long, deep breaths.
3. Begin the experiment by holding the chain or string of the pendulum in your dominant hand about 2 inches away from the dangling object or bobber.
4. Break the east-west motion by making a deliberate movement either clockwise or counterclockwise. Hold the pendulum over your other hand.
5. Ask yourself how the movement feels; does it feel natural? If not, hold the string or chain a bit higher and keep going until you find the position that feels right to you and allows the weight on the chain to rotate freely.
6. Mark that place with permanent marker or a straight pin.
7. Ask simple yes-or-no questions and start your dowsing session.
8. Be sure to make note of the answers and the day's date.

What sort of questions should you ask? Don't get into dark areas, and try to keep the questions simple. If you're looking for employment, you can start by asking, "Will I find work in the next three months?" If the answer is yes, then narrow it down even further. "Will I get work in the next month?" Don't ask complex questions that can't be answered properly with a simple yes or no, such as "How much money will the job pay?"

Predicting Events

In dowsing, as in so many things in life, practice makes perfect. Inevitably, people who have some luck at dowsing begin to ask for information about the future. Be aware of and guard yourself against the influence of negative responses. There is a real danger to those who are sensitive to negative news. Remember that the answers you get about future events are only possibilities and are not written in stone. Free will and corrective actions in the present can change what is still to come. In other words, if you don't like the answers you get, use your free will to make choices that will change the outcome.

Finding Your Balance

Making sense of your states of mind and all the methods of communicating with those on the other side can be difficult at first. Here is a suggestion to help you find an inner balance: Create a place in your mind where you can escape for a few moments, and learn to relax there. For some, this may seem impossible. If relaxing at this time is difficult for you, don't worry. As you progress through this book, you will learn how to find your balance.

You may already be familiar with the term *centering yourself*. Many situations in your life can keep you from being centered. You may be kept off balance by the people around you, the environment, or psychic information when it pours through the unconscious mind. It is easy to be overwhelmed by all the stimuli, both external and internal. To help deal with life's uncertainties, you need to learn how to center yourself.

EXERCISE: CONNECT WITH YOUR THIRD EYE

Your third eye, a spot of mental focus, is located between and above your two eyes in the center of your forehead. It is the point of connection to your sixth chakra, which is often associated with your pituitary gland (a small gland the size of a pea located at the base of your brain). All three of your eyes form the points of a triangle, a symbol that is found throughout ancient history, especially in the society of the pyramid builders. Perhaps they were aware of some now-lost secret that helped them connect to the eye of the soul.

Focus Upward

An easy way to center yourself is to make a connection with your third eye. If you have a religious background, you may choose to connect with your third eye when you pray. You can also do it through meditation. Another approach for connecting with your third eye is by doing the following exercise.

For a moment, look upward with your two physical eyes as if you were trying to see your third eye. If for some reason this is impossible or hard for you to do, that's okay; it is not actually necessary to move or see through your two eyes to experience this. You may keep your two eyes open or closed while you peek up under your eyelids. You may want to squint slightly and feel your third eye.

When you try this, you may feel a slight pressure in your third eye. It may feel like it is swelling or even vibrating. You may have a feeling of warmth or coolness, or you may perceive a certain color. Whatever you experience is okay—it's also possible that you won't feel anything at all.

Each person will connect to their third eye in a way that is natural and correct for them. Remember, there is no one else exactly like you. No one else will have the experience that you have when you communicate through your third eye.

Breathe

Now let's add something else to help you center yourself when you connect to your third eye. You may want to take a moment and find a comfortable place to sit or lie down. If any of your clothing is tight, you may want to loosen it a little. It is not absolutely necessary, but it may help you to become a little more centered. When you have done this, you may allow yourself to feel a connection with your third eye.

For a moment, allow yourself to get comfortable with the sensations you are experiencing as you make this connection. When you're ready, take a deep breath at a level that feels right for you. It may not be easy for you to inhale deeply, and that's okay. What is important is for you to breathe at a pace that helps you strengthen the connection with your third eye.

Continue to breathe slowly for a few minutes. It doesn't matter whether you keep your eyes open or closed—whatever way feels right for you is correct. Your mind may just drift away. It may also be very active, with lots of thoughts suddenly popping up, or it may focus on one thing.

MEDITATION FOR BEGINNERS

Some people get frustrated trying to learn to meditate. They are instructed to quiet their mind, but they find it impossible to do. If your mind is that way, don't worry about it; just breathe and focus on your third eye as best you can.

After you have experienced the results of this exercise for a length of time that is comfortable for you, take a deep breath. As you exhale, release the connection with your third eye and come back to the surface of your mind refreshed and relaxed. The more you practice this, the easier it will be to make a positive connection. Focusing on your third eye is a great way to begin connecting to your psychic mind.

Working with a Medium

As discussed in Chapter 4, even beginners are able to recognize simple messages from those on the other side after learning a few basic techniques. However, if you want to take your skills to the next level, you might want to think about working with a medium. Or, maybe you're sensing that you already have what it takes to be a medium yourself.

Types of Mediums

Mediumship is a process of communication between a person or persons from the earth plane (medium) and discarnate beings (entities without physical bodies). A medium is said to be sensitive to vibrations from the spirit world, enabling him to communicate with discarnate entities, including angels and guides. Because of this ability, mediums can facilitate communication between spirits and people who are not mediums.

Mediumship has been practiced for centuries and is still actively practiced in many parts of the world. Mediumship can be broadly divided into two main categories: physical and mental.

PHYSICAL MEDIUMSHIP

In this form of mediumship, spirits manipulate energy systems, and all those present in the medium's vicinity can observe the phenomenon. It was an important form of mediumship in the eighteenth and nineteenth centuries, when most well-known mediums demonstrated physical mediumship during séances. It is still practiced today in controlled environments and under supervision.

In some forms of physical mediumship, a chemical reaction is caused in the medium's body when she comes in contact with the spirit. The reaction is said to be centered in the medium's solar plexus, as opposed to the base of the brain, as in the case of mental mediumship. Here are some of the types of physical mediumship:

- **Raps:** Spirits are said to sometimes communicate through raps and knocks, answering simple yes-or-no questions with sounds that seem to be coming from somewhere in the room.

- **Materialization:** Spirit faces, hands, and complete physical forms are said to have materialized many times during séances. The most famous story of materialization is that of "Katie King," a spirit that is said to have materialized during sessions with English medium Florence Cook in the 1870s. Materialized entities are different from ghosts or apparitions and appear very rarely.

- **Apports and levitations:** An apport is the movement of a physical object, like a book or a flower, from one place to another by a spirit during a séance, or the sudden appearance of an item from an unknown source or location. Séances are not necessary to make apports occur; the spirit can transport the item anywhere or anytime if it so wishes. Mediums have also been known to levitate during séances. The most famous case of this involved the nineteenth-century Scottish medium Daniel Dunglas Home, who reportedly levitated out of a third-story window and then re-entered through a different window.

- **Direct voice:** These are audible voices of a paranormal nature produced during a séance. Trumpets were often used at séances to amplify the faint voices of the spirits; however, the voices can also be heard independent of any device. Several investigators recorded voice manifestations in séances conducted by twentieth-century British medium Leslie Flint.

MENTAL MEDIUMSHIP

In mental mediumship, also referred to as telepathic mediumship, communication occurs within the medium's consciousness without the involvement of the five physical senses. The following three types are the most popular:

- **Clairvoyance (clear seeing):** In the context of mediumship, clairvoyance refers to seeing images, people, or animals that may not be physically present or visible to non-mediums. In some cases, mediums may see a spirit standing before them, as if it were a physical entity. The images seen by mediums may have a symbolic meaning in relation to the spirit's life.

- **Clairsentience (clear feeling):** This is the ability of mediums to sense or experience the presence of a spirit. Many people experience this as the feeling that someone is behind them or that someone is staring at them. Mediums are just more sensitive and can pick up more details, such as feeling the touch of the spirit or a cold breeze blowing, smelling a scent or fragrance, or sensing the personality of the deceased.

- **Clairaudience (clear hearing):** This is the ability of mediums to hear spirit voices that are inaudible to non-mediums who may be present in the vicinity. Mediums have also reported hearing spoken thoughts, music, and singing.

Identifying a Spirit

Spirits have the burden of proving their identities. It would be nice if they simply stated their names; some do, but not always. If a spirit attempts to give its name, the medium may hear only one or two letters of it, which is usually enough to establish the correct name of the spirit. They send out all the right information; we simply are not tuned to receive it! They impart much more information in a variety of ways, such as by telling secrets, identifying objects, and even exposing causes of death, which may not always match what appears on the coroner's report. Many statements by spirits carry additional information that must be interpreted by the medium. It is the medium's challenge to gather the information and present it in a way that the intended recipient will understand the message.

Spirits communicate telepathically; they are accustomed to sending and receiving mental messages. Comparing their language to ours would be like putting into words what you did on your last vacation compared to the memories of the vacation that you see in your mind. Spirits vibrate at a higher frequency, which means they transmit more information in a shorter period of time than the living do. The medium receiving these messages must be capable of raising his vibration in order to understand the messages.

Whatever a spirit was best known for here on earth is most likely what he will project to the medium to validate his identity. There are many ways that a spirit's identity can be conveyed. One technique is to reference a medical condition. For example, if a person suffered a stroke and lost mobility on one side of his body, the medium may exhibit those same symptoms, such as slurred speech or leaning to one side. Once the condition is recognized as being specific to the spirit, the symptoms and the condition disappear; the medium returns to normal.

Séance: A Group Event

The word *séance* comes from the Old French word *seoir*, meaning "to sit." A séance is an event during which a medium communicates with the deceased. It is believed that during the event the spirits are enabled to visit the location where the séance is being held. In some cases, the medium leading the communication is used as a vehicle for the spirits to directly communicate with those present. In others, the spirits may make their presence known via smells, sounds, or touch. In rare cases, participants in a séance have also reported spirit sightings.

SÉANCES THROUGH THE AGES

Man has been attempting to communicate with those who have passed beyond since time immemorial. But in modern times it was the Fox sisters, Margaret and Kate, who were perhaps the first acknowledged and famed for their ghostly encounters. In the late 1840s, the girls communicated with a spirit in their haunted home using a series of claps and knocks to get answers to their questions. They went on to publicly demonstrate their spiritual powers.

MESSAGES FROM THE OTHER SIDE

Paschal Beverly Randolph conducted famous séances in the nineteenth century. Randolph would act as a messenger between his audience and the spirits they wished to talk to. Another famous spiritualist was the medium Leafy Anderson, who, in the early 1900s, contacted the spirit of Black Hawk, a Native American warrior who died in 1838.

Séances were popularized in the second half of the nineteenth century thanks to the rise of spiritualism, a belief that the spirits of the dead can communicate with the living. When spiritualism first arose as a religion and grew into a movement, many self-styled mediums and spirit communicators emerged from various sections of society. They brought news of the dead, including where they were and whether or not they were happy. Inevitably, many fraudsters took advantage of the mystic nature of these spiritual activities and made money off gullible believers who were desperate to communicate with deceased loved ones.

Although many mediums and several well-publicized séances came to be exposed as frauds later on, there were still many others that held up under the closest scrutiny. Today séances continue to open the doors between our world and the beyond. Believers come together and combine their spiritual energies to call for spirits to visit them.

DIFFERENT KINDS OF SÉANCES

The movement of spiritualism encouraged communication with the dead to learn about the world beyond our understanding and the afterlife and to prove the continuity of life itself. In public séances, which were usually held in spiritualist churches or camps, spiritualist ministers conveyed messages from the dead to living members of the congregation. At times, a particularly receptive medium would function as the messenger instead of an ordained minister. These public religious services continue today throughout the world and usually contain healing services as well as lectures on various spiritual topics.

Group Séances
In group séances, a number of believers come together at one location to communicate with the spirits. Each one may have a question to

ask the otherworld's visitors. The leader of the group séance needs to be a very sensitive medium in order to establish a successful contact with a spirit.

The medium may slip into a trancelike state, allowing the spirits to communicate through him. At other times the information may be related verbally without any sign of interaction between the medium and the recipients. Sometimes the medium communicates the spirit's message through automatic writing. Spirits can also communicate through sounds like knocking or scratching.

Spiritual Circles

Smaller groups of people who are interested in exploring supernatural phenomena conduct séances in the hope of learning more about the otherworld. These spiritual circle séances are more exploratory in nature, and often the participants do not have any specific questions or wish to contact a particular spirit. However, they do wish to expand their knowledge of the process and hopefully develop their own mediumistic abilities.

Séances with Manifestations

When spiritualism was at its peak, many mediums claimed an ability to generate ectoplasmic manifestations of spirits. In these séances, participants could see a translucent shape issue from the medium. It was believed that this ectoplasm was a spirit in physical form. There were other reported manifestations, such as the transfiguration of the medium himself. Transfiguration and physical mediumship are still practiced today.

SÉANCE TOOLS

Many mediums offer themselves as the vehicle for the spirit to communicate with the living. Others use special tools to comprehend what the spirit is trying to convey. Ouija boards, or spirit boards, are widely used to understand messages from the spirit world. Some mediums also use trumpets to hear the spirits talk or slates where the spirits can leave written messages. Sometimes mediums also confine themselves in spirit cabinets from which they emerge with messages from the otherworld.

SÉANCES—ARE THEY REAL?

The existence of paranormal entities like spirits and the possibility of communicating with them through séances have been questioned repeatedly by skeptics and scientists. Famed magician and illusionist Harry Houdini duplicated many of the famous séances conducted during his lifetime and exposed them as illusions. However, Houdini was also a firm believer in the paranormal and often made his beliefs public.

Several well-known scientists and inventors, including Sir William Crookes, Alexander Graham Bell, and Guglielmo Marconi, firmly believed in the power of séances to reach paranormal entities. Marconi went so far as to attempt a direct communication with spirits using radio signals.

Science has evolved over the years to produce explanations for many of our ancestors' unsolved mysteries. But there are still many paranormal phenomena, including afterlife communication, that are beyond the reach of science today. It's up to you to review the available information and decide for yourself.

Signs from the Other Side

When a loved one passes away, it leaves a big hole in your life. Not only is the grief immense, but your life also changes in a big way. Some people are completely shattered by such unfortunate incidents in their lives. But if you believe in the existence of the soul after death, the idea that your loved one is not entirely lost can give you some emotional and mental relief. Seeing signs from that loved one might help you cope with your grief.

The Need for Contact

Communicating with the dead is said to expand your consciousness to higher levels. When you tune in to the frequencies of the spiritual world, you can experience and feel things beyond the material world. You channel energies of the otherworld and enter into realms of larger consciousness. Spirits of deceased loved ones are said to facilitate such experiences.

Believers in the afterlife strongly advocate making such contacts with your departed to feel closer to them and also to become more educated about the mysterious yet powerful alternate world of spirits. Some people have even postulated that the dead feel the need to make contact with their loved ones in the material world. This may be to offer solace or to make the presence of the afterlife and the alternate world felt. More and more researchers and doctors today agree on the positive effects of after-death contact. It can be stress relieving and may give new meaning to a person's life after a tragedy. Following are some reasons a loved one might try to contact you.

ALLEVIATION OF GRIEF AFTER THE LOSS OF A LOVED ONE

Many grief and bereavement studies on after-death contact have revealed that the bereaved person usually finds it easier to accept and cope with the loss of a loved one after experiencing contact. Many feel that being able to contact the deceased serves to dilute the unfinished business or suddenness of loss. The continuity of the person's existence in another form after death eases the sense of loss and also gives a feeling of accessibility to the departed person.

In 1995, Allan Botkin, a clinical psychologist specializing in post-traumatic stress disorder, reportedly discovered a method of inducing after-death contact for his bereaved and grieving patients. He claimed that the experience induced by this methodology left the subjects feeling relieved and closer to their deceased loved ones. However, critics of such methods say that such experiences can negatively affect people and leave them even more disturbed.

EMOTIONAL SOLACE AND EXPRESSION OF LOVE/CARING

In many after-death contacts, the deceased are observed communicating messages meant to impart solace, such as "I'm okay," "I love you," "Don't worry about me," "Go on with your life," and "I'm watching over you." The spirits seem to want to confirm their continued existence and express love for those they left behind, while granting their loved ones permission to move on. Such comforting words can be healing for the grieving person. It can give you the strength to gather the pieces of your life and feel at peace with your and your deceased's existence in different worlds.

SPIRITS SIMPLIFY LIFE

Many times spirits just want to communicate that they have "made it" to the other side and that they still exist and are not in any pain. The drama in our daily lives does not interest them, as they seem to see the bigger picture of the meaning of life, which is love.

The spirits of the departed might try to establish contact with their loved ones through signs to continue the emotional and spiritual bond that they share with them. Their goal is to remind you of the continuing relationship they have with you, though the modes of communication may have changed since death. It is hypothesized that spirits exist at a higher vibrational frequency than living beings in the material world. In order to establish contact, both the spirit and the receiver have to adjust their frequencies to find a common ground where they can communicate.

CLOSURE/SOLVING A MYSTERY

Many of us would leave no stone unturned if we lost a loved one as the result of an unsolved mystery or crime. Evidence can be vague, unpredictable, unreliable, and often inaccurate. A witness may withhold certain information for personal protection, whereas a spirit wants to divulge all of the facts. If the obvious is being overlooked, the spirit tends to be more forceful. A spirit may repeat the same message to many people, hoping that one person will grasp the answer to the challenging conundrum.

Naming Suspects

Spirits may come through and actually name the perpetrator. Or they may give one hint at a time, as in a scavenger hunt, until the person receiving the information puts the pieces together. Spirits are focused on telling the truth. They will accept the responsibility if they were the cause of their own death.

MESSAGES FROM THE OTHER SIDE

Two years after a woman was murdered, her parents came to medium Joseph M. Higgins for a session. They did not believe that she had been killed by an unknown intruder during a break-in. Higgins was able to confirm that the murder weapon was a baseball bat. The daughter told him that the break-in was staged and that her husband had committed the crime. While the husband was a person of interest, there was not enough evidence for the authorities to charge him.

The daughter cautioned her parents to back off and communicated that in twelve months' time, her husband would be charged with the crime and serve time in prison. She did not want her parents to impede the police investigation. The parents agreed, as they trusted their daughter's message. One year later, Higgins received a call from the family informing him that the husband had been arrested and charged with the daughter's murder, and was serving time in prison.

When Is the Best Time to Look for Signs?

The best time to attempt contact is when your mind is at ease and your body relaxed. The largest obstacle to communication with the other side is interference from outside sources, so choose a time when there are minimal outside stimuli grabbing your attention. These stimuli can be the overall activity surrounding you, or even things that are on your mind and have kept you occupied throughout the day.

Whether or not communication is successful also depends on how open you are to receiving contact from a deceased loved one. These are important issues that have to be addressed first before an attempt can be made.

A particularly good time for a connection is when you are just waking up from a sound sleep or perhaps a daytime nap, as many of your burdens, worries, and random thoughts are pushed to the side, making it easier for a sign, a contact, to come through.

PROBABILITY AND STATISTICAL EVIDENCE

The big question is, how do you know if the signs you are observing are truly from your departed loved ones? Renowned after-death communication (ADC) researchers and authors of *Hello from Heaven!*, Bill Guggenheim and Judy Guggenheim, interviewed 2,000 people of varying backgrounds between 1988 and 1995 across the United States and Canada and recorded more than 3,300 firsthand accounts of ADC with deceased friends or family members. All such recorded incidents were unaided by any medium, hypnotist, or device.

Common Ways Contact Is Made

Some surveys say that over 20 percent of the U.S. population has encountered an after-death communication (ADC). A majority of people have the ability to recognize signs coming from the other side, but most brush off these experiences as flukes or wishful thinking. It may not be their intention to make the connection more difficult, but this is often the result. It is up to the receiver to be able to pick up the sometimes subtle hints that communication is taking place.

There are numerous methods for achieving ADC, but the communication process is not limited to these methods. Spirits have vast interacting abilities within the physical plane. All you need to receive these messages is an open mind to the possibility and understanding if no sign is to come.

LOOK FOR ANY TYPE OF SIGN

When you ask for a sign from the other side, it is important to then be willing to accept any communication that comes through. Do not be so quick to dismiss coincidences, as these might be the actual signs that you have requested.

SMELLS AND SOUNDS

Studies have shown that distinct memories can be associated with a smell or a sound. Childhood memories are filled with the smells of your favorite foods on holidays and special occasions. Perhaps it's the smell of the leather of a baseball glove or the distinct odor of a favorite relative's perfume. Many remember a favorite song or concert that they attended. Smells and sounds are two of the strongest methods that spirits use to get the attention of a person in the physical plane. Your connection to these methods has been developed over your entire life and is easily accessed to get a message through.

NATURE

Many people have a close relationship with the natural surroundings of the physical plane. Within these boundaries are methods of contact that can be arranged to show a sign. Spirits have the ability to intercede in the action of the animal world, as well as with plants and the weather. If someone would recognize a sign more easily through the action of an animal or perhaps a significant flower or breeze, then this would be implemented in the spirit's choice of contact.

For some people, the sounds of nature are used, as these bring back many fond memories of departed loved ones and can be relaxing at the same time. The sound of the wind blowing through the trees, raindrops hitting the ground, or the ocean crashing on a beach are examples of natural sounds that can be used to draw your attention toward a message about a passed loved one.

PHYSICAL SENSATIONS

Many subjects experiencing ADC report feeling a physical sensation of touch, like a toss of the hair, a pressing on the shoulders, or a brush against the cheek.

TELEPATHY OR HEARING A VOICE

Some people also get messages from the deceased through either telepathy or an external voice. For example, people have reported hearing the deceased's voice on a telephone after the phone rang.

DREAMS

Sigmund Freud believed that dreams were a means of expressing repressed thought. But today, due to advancements in science, dreams are thought to be the product of the brain and the still-misunderstood concept of consciousness. Could it be a combination of both of these theories? Could it be a doorway to the other side that we can tap into for cross-communications?

The dream state is used to communicate more complex messages that would be difficult to send during the waking state. While awake, most people are overwhelmed with stimuli from many different sources. Most have pressing responsibilities, and with them as a distraction, it can be difficult to receive complex messages. These messages can be sent through either one-way or two-way communication between the deceased and the receiver.

What Are Astral Dreams?

Regardless of whether we remember them, we all have astral dreams, or "visits," as they're sometimes called. Our departed loved ones and our personal spirit guides, who help us with life choices, actually visit with us. Because there are no limits to space or time in the dream or spirit world, we can find ourselves walking along the Seine in Paris with an old friend who died several years ago, or in Alaska, dogsledding with Great-Granddad.

Here are two ways to recognize a true astral dream.

1. First, the events in astral dreams, like in prophetic dreams, happen in a sequential order.

2. Second, spirits are usually happy with where they are, and they want you to know that. If for some reason you feel in your dream that a spirit is evil, or even just sad or angry, you are probably combining a release dream with an astral visit.

DON'T REJECT AN ASTRAL DREAM

A release dream can kick in when you have an astral visit from someone you love who has died. Out of fear, grief, or shock, you may push him away in your dream, even though he's trying to tell you he's okay. Spirits are usually happy beings! Dreamers are the ones who are afraid.

Stages of Sleep

Learning about the stages of sleep can help you understand how and when an astral visit might occur.

1. **Stage 1:** This lasts for only a few minutes and is very light sleep. The person can be easily woken up by outside disturbances.

2. **Stage 2:** This is a much deeper sleep than the first stage. Dreams begin in this stage, with unclear images and vague thoughts drifting in the person's mind. However, outside disturbances will break the sleep even at this stage.

3. **Stage 3:** Muscles become relaxed now and blood pressure, heart rate, and breathing become slow and even. Waking a

person in this stage is difficult. Only repeated calling of the person's name or a loud noise can awaken him.

4. **REM State:** This is the state when all dreams occur, as it is the deepest state of sleep. It is difficult to wake a person in this state. Here, blood pressure and heart rate fluctuate and rapid eye movement (REM) takes place. This state, also known as the REM state, lasts for about ten minutes. Then the person goes back into deep sleep, or the non-rapid eye movement (NREM) state. The cycle continues, alternating between the REM and NREM states.

The best way to identify an astral dream is to keep a pen and piece of paper near your bedside. When you wake up in the middle of the night, first thing in the morning, or from a daydream and you remember something that's significant, write it down.

The Visit Itself

Carl Jung, the founder of analytical psychology, said, "Dreams have a psychic structure which is unlike that of other contents of consciousness." He also described how some dreams seem prophetic in nature, or telepathic. The other side is always trying to make contact through the dream state. It is much easier for spirits to tap into the subconscious state at that level. The dream state is a "communication connector," a highway that is wide open, unburdened by outside conflicting stimuli. As soon as you reach your dream state, contact can begin.

Communication can be visual, meaning you can see them and they can see you. Many people can remember encountering relatives and friends in their dreams. They can connect with you through speech and sound; you might relive or enjoy a moment together in a world that is as solid as the one where you currently exist.

HOW TO TELL A REGULAR DREAM FROM AN ASTRAL DREAM

You may remember that the colors are more vivid, the sounds are more pronounced, and you may feel that you recognize the people you see. You know instinctively that it is different from one of your ordinary dreams. These are all clues that you have actually tapped into the other side of existence.

Daydreaming

Daydreaming is a state that is not only healthy, but also an opportunity for the other side to step in and give insight and instruction you might need at that time. This state, in which your mind wanders from thought to thought, is very similar to meditation; thoughts slow down and your mind begins to wander without focusing on any particular thing at any particular point. This opening allows for the sharing of creative ideas, problem-solving techniques, and other forms of information that may be needed or wanted at that time.

Clairvoyant Dreams

Parapsychologists like Charles Tart believe that dreams are entry points into another realm. Clairvoyant dreams or prophetic dreams are those that seem to foretell the future. Some claim that dreams are gateways to past lives; others say they are ways of gaining knowledge and understanding complex ideas. Many creative expressions, such as music and inventions, have been formulated in the dream and day-dream states.

According to medium Joseph M. Higgins, you must first understand the possibility and means of communicating with the other side. "Since the beginning of time," he says, "dreams have been the most efficient and easiest way for them to communicate with you." So sleep well, keep an open mind, and enjoy the conversation.

SYNCHRONICITY

A synchronicity is a meaningful coincidence that relates to the deceased, like spotting the person's name in an unexpected place, hearing the person's favorite song right after you thought about him, and so on. An object used to get your attention will make you take notice and recognize that the departed is trying to connect with you. If you had a family member who drove a big black Cadillac or had a coin collection, then these are the objects that a loved one would likely use to gain your attention. There are literally hundreds of different objects that can be presented to you as signs provided by your loved ones.

Some common signs of synchronicity are:

- Certain birds, like cardinals, owls, and crows
- Rainbows
- Cloud formations
- License plates
- Butterflies
- Ladybugs

- Songs
- Heart shapes found in everyday objects

NO TIME OR SPACE

Once again, remember that there is no time or space on the other side. If you're receiving any information about the future from a departed loved one (though this is rare), be sure to record it. But remember that something that seems as if it could happen tomorrow might actually happen twenty years from now.

Objects will mean different things to different individuals, depending on the relationship to the one who is being contacted. Therefore, a baseball bat might mean nothing to one person, but it could be the perfect object to use to communicate with someone else whose loved one played baseball throughout his entire life.

You might want to start writing down the synchronicities that you notice throughout the day. As you keep track, you'll likely start to find patterns and actually observe synchronicities more frequently! Reviewing your notes from months ago will also bring a smile to your face when you need a pick-me-up.

APPORTS: THE MATERIALIZATION OF MATTER

As mentioned in Chapter 5, the astonishing and mysterious materialization of an object out of thin air, or its movement from one place to another, is called an "apport." Apports often are associated with spiritual séances and mediumship, but they can and do happen outside of these events, and might even occur during one's daily life. For example, have you ever lost your keys, a piece of jewelry, or a cell phone and then found the missing item in a place you could swear you already looked?

MISSING ITEMS

Sure, the probability of someone misplacing an object and then finding it in the same place is rather high, as multitasking and the responsibilities of daily living cause many to lose track of their belongings. But there are also occasions when an apport could be the reason for that maddening search.

Often the object is one that triggers fond memories of the loved one who has passed to the other side. It could be a family heirloom, a recent gift, or an object that is presented to you that reminds you of the person you were thinking about. Sometimes the object is physically placed where you will notice it, but most often the spirit will direct your attention to a location that you might have overlooked. With this method of contact, the spirit uses the emotions attached to a particular object to get your attention.

The phenomenon of apportation is considered exceptional and one of a kind. While many instances of apports have been proven to be fraudulent, apport mediums have demonstrated the phenomenon to audiences of skeptics, researchers, and medical professionals under highly supervised conditions. With no signs of fraud evident, researchers have been stumped to explain the phenomenon.

Nineteenth-century German astrophysicist Johann Zöllner put forward the theory of a fourth dimension to explain the phenomenon. He suggested that the objects were lifted into this fourth dimension, where they were manipulated before being returned. It has been proposed that psychics possess a four-dimensional way of seeing and perceiving things, which is a higher order of experience than that of the general non-medium/non-psychic population.

The theories proposed are breathtaking, as they require a whole new perspective and a different, more open-minded view of spiritual or psychic phenomena. Those who have not experienced the phenomenon of apportation may find it hard to imagine a fourth dimension or the superior powers of apport mediums, but those from the scientific community who have experienced and researched the phenomenon are convinced of its paranormal nature. Through the study of quantum physics and string theory, the idea of multiple dimensions does not seem as far-fetched as researchers once thought.

MESSAGES FROM THE OTHER SIDE

People going about their daily routines have reported feathers floating down upon them, within a closed space or home, when the thought of a loved one entered their minds. This phenomenon has been witnessed by friends and family members, and has no explanation.

How Do You Know If the Signs Are Real?

This is the question often asked by skeptics and those observing signs from their deceased loved ones. The answer may lie in the probability of the event happening.

When you observe a sign, think about the probability of the occurrence of the event. What is the likelihood of it happening? If the event is highly unlikely and yet it has occurred, it may be a case of after-death communication (ADC).

Many people also observe signs on a recurring basis, such as the placement of an object in a particular way or in a particular place every day/week/month, or spotting some animals in an uncharacteristic fashion several times. There are also others who observe several signs in quick succession. Such incidents suggest that such signs may not be mere coincidences but attempts of contact by the deceased.

Carl Jung said that such "meaningful coincidences" or "signs" cannot always be traced to a casual relationship. Many of these may be connected to some unexplainable, "acausal" principle. He called this "synchronicity" (discussed earlier in this chapter). Though many scholars have debated this idea, there are some who stand by it and agree that such events could be triggered by forces beyond our understanding.

Animal Reactions to Human Death

Countless people have experienced the loss of a dear pet that has become a close companion or member of the family. However, what happens when a pet loses its owner? Are animals capable of not only sensing but mourning their loss as well? If a pet recently faced with the death of its owner acts oddly, is it possible it's sensing or seeing its deceased owner's spirit? This section will examine the possibility that animals' exceptional senses grant them a gateway into the paranormal that humans cannot access.

It's common knowledge that animals possess senses that are far superior to humans'. Yet, according to Linda Cole in her article "Can Pets See Ghosts?" it seems that their senses are so finely tuned that they can perceive paranormal activity that humans are not able to. She also comments on animals' astounding senses in her inquisitive article, debating whether animals are seeing ghosts or merely behaving oddly:

> "Compared to us, our pets have phenomenal senses we can't come close to. Their hearing is far superior to ours. They can sniff out cancer in people and find hidden explosives. They know, sometimes hours before we do, that a storm is brewing and they need little light to navigate around the furniture in the living room."

Most find the concept that animals are capable of seeing ghosts utterly ridiculous and dismiss the notion without further consideration. But the fact remains that numerous people have witnessed odd, inexplicable behavior in their pets, like a dog staring intensely at a deceased owner's empty chair, then barking and acting in an agitated manner, or a cat reaching out and batting the air.

There are many mysteries to life we can't explain and there's no definitive testing we can use to prove that ghosts share our dimension. Pets, on the other hand, don't try to analyze or examine evidence. They see what they see. If pets really can see ghosts, the only way they can tell us is by their head and eye movements or odd behavior as they follow something through a room or up a staircase.

Clearly, there are processes at work in the universe undetectable to the human eye, ear, nose, and tactile sensitivity. However, animals exhibit outward signs of grief when their owners pass away that their new caretakers can easily observe.

PETS FEEL GRIEF TOO

Bereavement, grief, mourning, and deep-seated emotions are not foreign to pets that suffer the loss of their owner. Numerous caretakers have observed the acute distress that afflicts animals in the absence of their friend, companion, and teacher.

Despite the fact that it cannot be proven, the notion that animals may be capable of detecting the presence of a paranormal being, such as a spirit or ghost, is made possible by examining their far superior senses and noting inexplicable behaviors. Pets are commonly considered members of the family and like any familial element, they react to the loss of a cherished companion with depression, anxiety, and possibly the sense that their deceased owner's spirit has lingered behind and is still with them.

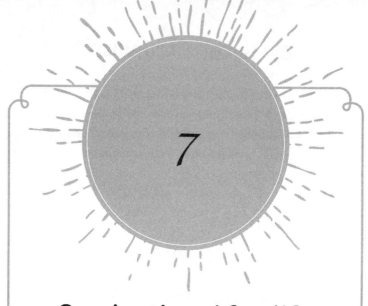

Conducting Afterlife Experiments

It is always fascinating to read about the research and investigations into the afterlife. Weighing the evidence of such a realm is a daunting task. But with modern-day technology, it is now possible for anyone to conduct her own look into this complex and mysterious subject. If you're into gadgets and data, you'll love this opportunity to measure temperatures, take video, and track spiritual contact. The first and most important thing to have? A commitment to learning with an open mind.

Laying the Groundwork

The best way to learn about anything is to actually do it. If you have read everything you can get your hands on about paranormal events and the technical aspects of ghost hunting, talked to people about the supernatural, and joined discussion forums online, you may be ready to start doing a little more technical investigating on your own.

JOIN THE HUNT

The easiest and fastest way to start investigating is to join a group already in progress. Ask around your community about paranormal groups that meet regularly. Try to find individuals who have developed a reputation as psychic or paranormal investigators. Call or write and introduce yourself. Set up an appointment to meet them and see if you can arrange to go on a ghost hunt.

Most groups that perform paranormal investigations have a form they ask prospective members to fill out. They do this to be sure you understand the responsibilities, possible danger, and/or legal issues involved in paranormal investigation. This form frees them from legal liability should anything happen to you in the course of the investigation. You will also be briefed and made familiar with the group's procedures and investigative techniques. It is likely you will be put on probation until the training is completed. This is to ensure that you understand all the possible ramifications of your actions should something unexpected occur.

TRAINING AND PROBATION

A good organization should expose you to, and train you in, the tools of the trade as they are defined today. You may show an affinity for one particular tool, such as a dowsing rod or digital camera. If you find that you're particularly adept at something, try to develop your expertise in it; the group will appreciate having someone who is highly skilled and motivated. No two researchers are the same, and everyone's skill levels will vary.

A calm demeanor and good observational skills are essential. If you can remain objective and are keenly aware of your surroundings, you will be an invaluable asset to any group you join. If you have any natural psychic ability, you can work on developing your sensitivity and skills in that area. A sort of natural on-the-job training in this area occurs as a result of the feedback you receive on an investigation.

Low-Tech Investigating Devices

Whether you join a group or investigate on your own, there are some basic tools you can use when tracking spirits. In order to prove the existence of the paranormal, investigators use both conventional and scientific devices.

Sometimes the simple low-tech tools are the ones people underestimate. If you have a limited budget, some of these devices can be better choices than their high-price counterparts in the short term. When batteries drain and electronic devices fail, even those who have high-tech gear may be very glad they brought along their low-tech backup. If you are not technologically savvy or simply do not want to fuss with a lot of equipment, low-tech is the way to go.

LIGHTING EQUIPMENT

There's nothing more important than being able to see during an investigation, and since most investigations take place at night, having a flashlight, spotlight, or lantern on hand is absolutely essential. Also, since spirits are supposed to take energy from the sources available, according to paranormal researchers, the flashlight may go off in the middle of an investigation. At least one backup and an extra supply of batteries may be useful.

LED keychain lights that can hang from a lanyard around your neck are always handy—plus they can be left on for a hands-free way of lighting one's feet in the darkness. Battery-powered lighted pens have small lights that allow you to write in the dark. If batteries are being drained, glow sticks provide an easy and cheap solution.

Flashlights

Flashlights are an essential, basic item for any investigator. Investigators should have a red filter fitted to the lens or a red bulb. The red-tinted light keeps night vision intact and eyes adjusted to lower light levels. Lots of extra batteries are also essential.

Headlamps and Spotlights

Small battery-powered headlamps may be extremely helpful when you need your hands free to take pictures or read data. Not as obtrusive as a spotlight, these lights allow investigators to hold other equipment and move about more freely.

Battery-operated spotlights are very helpful in areas with no power. They make setting up and breaking down equipment so much easier.

Lanterns

Flashlights have their place, but batteries can drain quickly. Kerosene lanterns can provide light when flashlights die. Although they are more cumbersome and expensive than the average flashlight, they can be enormously helpful.

COMPASSES

Simple in both construction and function, the compass is probably the most overlooked yet dependable paranormal tool in existence. The humble compass is a highly useful electromagnetic field (EMF) sensor. It has largely been replaced by more accurate and sensitive electronics, but this paranormal tool is still used by many investigation traditionalists and those who wish to have a dependable backup to their modern-day electronic equipment. Compass needles can be moved by energies with a strong EMF that may well be paranormal in origin.

ADVENTURE PAPER

This waterproof, tear-resistant paper can stand up to difficult field conditions. Sold mostly in outdoor outfitter stores, this paper is made by National Geographic. It works well for printing out anything that may be subject to the elements, such as maps, directions, and field notes.

WATCHES

A reliable timepiece is an essential bit of equipment for keeping track of time spent during the investigation and to help coordinate the team's efforts. While many use cell phones to keep track of the time, keep in mind that the battery can drain quickly. A hand-wound analog watch that has no batteries may be a great backup.

DOWSING RODS

Dowsing rods are Y- or L-shaped twigs or metal rods used in tandem to detect objects. Some researchers feel that the use of dowsing rods can help to pick up a paranormal presence; however, not everyone has luck with dowsing rods, even in ordinary circumstances. These are best used by those with proven dowsing ability.

Basic Ghost Hunting Technology

Capturing a spirit's presence via sound, photography, temperature changes, or video is probably your ultimate goal. Following is more information about tools to gather those types of data.

STILL PHOTOGRAPHY

A picture is worth a thousand words. That's never truer than when it is applied to pictures of the paranormal. Although in the digital age people may tend to be suspicious of all images in general and ghost photos in particular, it is still truly stunning to see video or still photos of apparitions or ghosts. Although most teams now use digital cameras, there are those who assert that film cameras actually provide better views. If you use a digital camera, be sure to use one with as high a resolution as possible. As technology improves, the limits of image capture size will keep increasing. Any camera that has the capacity of shooting at three megapixels or above is fine, be it a cell phone or a regular digital camera. Obviously a camera will have more storage capacity, a better lens, and a better zoom, but some smartphones capture remarkably good images. Save images at as high a resolution as possible, and if you enhance a photo, save the original and work on a copy.

COLLECTING PARANORMAL IMPRINTS

Try flattening a piece of Play-Doh and leaving it in an area of possible paranormal phenomena or when trying to contact the other side. Look at it later to see if any physical imprints have been left in it. Make sure to record your findings, as you may want to try it again under different circumstances.

Researcher and author David Rountree has been investigating since the 1970s. He has a science background and a master's degree in electronic engineering in digital signal processing and has written extensively on the use of science and technology to properly investigate the paranormal. He believes there is a place for both digital and analog cameras in the field, but that digital may have an edge because "Nearly all digital cameras use the same type imaging chip. This chip 'sees' well into the infrared and ultraviolet spectrum, the two extreme ends of the light spectrum." Rountree says that UV light is so effective in photographing paranormal activity that a cottage industry has sprung up of folks specializing in removing the filters on digital cameras to make them full-spectrum cameras, or to add filters to them to make them into infrared (IR) or UV cameras.

RAW Digital Files Lend Authenticity

More high-end digital cameras offer a format known as "raw." These files are uncompressed, and any anomalous raw image that is examined using this format can be easily authenticated. Preserving the original and only enhancing such things as contrast and exposure on the copy is essential.

Cameras Provide Complete Data

A bonus feature of digital files is that vital information is embedded within them. This vital information can tell you about the camera make and model, the date and time the image was shot, what camera settings were used, whether flash was used, and the ISO settings. If image data is changed or manipulated, the exchangeable image file (EXIF) records this information as well. You can easily analyze a digital image to see if it has been manipulated.

Do My Eyes Deceive Me?

Occasionally, cameras capture spectral mists and fogs during an investigation. Experienced ghost hunters know these mysterious mists are often caused by exhaled breath on a cold day or someone's cigarette smoke. Since no one should be smoking during an investigation, hopefully the latter can be ruled out as the cause of the fog. For the most part, when these eerie mists appear in photos, they were not visible to the naked eye when the pictures were snapped.

So what are you seeing? By following good paranormal investigative protocol, you will perhaps have enough other evidence to help understand what has transpired if such a picture shows up during one of your investigations.

If the ambient temperature in the room remained constant but you encountered cold spots or sudden temperature drops, then there is an increased likelihood that something paranormal was captured in your photos. If you have no other supporting evidence, whether such anomalous images represent genuine ghosts or anything paranormal will very likely be in dispute.

AUDIO RECORDERS

Recorders are small devices that pack lots of investigative punch and can be extremely useful and inexpensive investigative tools for ghost hunters. In fact, they are so indispensable and affordable that they are recommended as an essential part of any paranormal toolkit. The technology is advancing so quickly that it is a good idea to check back frequently at online stores to see if prices have dropped or capabilities have grown for a recorder.

Should you use old-fashioned tape recorders or the newer digital technology for investigations? The sound quality of digital recorders is excellent, and digital files are easily copied and transferred. However, some investigators prefer the older analog recorders that use tape, asserting they give a better sound quality. Whichever option you choose, an external microphone really adds clarity to the recordings. The reason is that the microphone is away from the machine and so will not record the internal noise of the recorder's operations.

TESLA AND THE OTHER SIDE

Nikola Tesla was an electronics genius whose early radio receivers reportedly picked up organized, intelligent signals during a time when the only functioning radio transmitter was Guglielmo Marconi's. Tesla studied the phantom signals and speculated they might originate from another planet—or even the spirit world. There were claims that he invented a so-called Teslascope for the purpose of communicating with spirits or extraterrestrials.

Audio and Electronic Voice Phenomena

Using both tape and digital voice recorders is standard practice in paranormal investigations. They are used to record interviews with witnesses and voice messages from the spirit world. Electronic voice phenomena (EVPs) are of particular interest to serious investigators. EVPs are unexplained audio events that can sometimes be heard as they are happening but far more often go unheard until the recording is played back during evidence review.

Capturing EVPs

The EVPs on recordings are often distinctive voices, talking in regional accents and dialects. Sometimes they have such an eerie quality that it is hard to listen to them. Some seem to struggle to get the words out, as if communicating over vast distances. They often call researchers by name. Some may even answer questions about their names or history. That sort of exchange is very exciting for investigators, particularly if they can substantiate some of the information.

MESSAGES FROM THE OTHER SIDE

Related to EVPs, a PCFTD is a phone call from the dead. For decades, people have reported receiving telephone calls from deceased family members and friends. Many of the reports are similar—a person receives a phone call late at night, and although the connection is bad, the recipient can recognize the caller's voice. When the recipient of the call makes a reference to the person being dead, the call abruptly ends.

Three types of devices are commonly used:

1. **Microcassette recorders:** These analog recorders use micro audiotapes.

2. **Digital voice recorders:** Tiny and inconspicuous with no tape, these digital recorders have great sound quality. Files from these devices can be uploaded to computers for analysis and audio cleanup. Files can also be emailed or posted on websites.

3. **Wireless microphones:** An often overlooked tool for paranormal research, these devices are growing in popularity. The wireless microphone allows users to record audio straight

to the hard drive of a computer, virtually eliminating background noise. Most kits include a microphone, transmitter, and receiver.

NIGHT VISION EQUIPMENT

Night vision goggles or even adapters that can be attached to your camera are particularly useful to see in the dark, so that one does not mistake a shadow for a spirit. If you have plenty of cash to spend on gear, quality night vision devices are a great choice. They are very expensive but also durable and incredibly useful. They eliminate the need for flashlights to light the way, which enables investigators to travel through completely lightless areas safely. Military surplus stores are a good source for this sort of equipment.

INFRARED THERMAL SCANNER

This tool measures temperature fluctuations by sending out a thermal beam. Paranormal investigators are able to locate "hot" and "cold" spots, which might be caused by paranormal activity.

WALKIE-TALKIES OR HEADSETS

When working in a group it is better to have walkie-talkies to keep in touch with the various members of the group or in case of an emergency. Teams may find the convenience of headset communicators quite useful to stay in touch with one another. Headset communicators, unlike walkie-talkies, allow users to go hands-free, which is always an asset when trying to juggle other equipment, such as meters and cameras.

More Advanced Ghost Hunting Equipment

Modern equipment is used more for ruling out the possibility of a discarnate being. While it does not indicate the presence of a supernatural being, it helps us to understand the scientific reason for some occurrences, thereby ruling out the possibility of anything surreal.

You do not really need all the gadgets listed here to carry out a paranormal investigation. Individuals who are into ghost hunting as a hobby and are not into advanced research and investigation can begin very simply, with as little gear as a light source, compass, voice recorder, and camera.

MEASURE YOUR BASELINES

Some of the best equipment you can have at your disposal is not specifically geared toward ghost detection at all. Devices that measure relative humidity, ambient temperature, voltage, airflow, decibel levels, and light sensitivity are extremely important for assessing the environment and how it may affect people physiologically. This should be done beforehand and at regular intervals during an investigation so you have multiple points of reference.

The following high-tech equipment is used by professional investigators. Some of it is new and in the early stages of experimentation but yielding interesting results:

- **Eight-camera CCTV system:** This ensemble allows the investigator to monitor eight areas at the same time continuously for three to four days. It also has a built-in recorder to make instant footage of what needs to be focused on or studied further.

- **Thermal imager:** This device is different from a thermometer in that there is no need for physical contact to measure the temperature changes. It produces images that we can see by measuring the difference in heat from a distance using the upper portion of the infrared spectrum. Spirits are believed to emit radiations in this frequency, and the imager is used for capturing that heat variation. Designed so the user can easily see and then analyze heat signatures, this device analyzes hot and cold atmospheric anomalies instantly. A thermal imager is considered one of the most sophisticated, ultimate tools for paranormal research, and it's probably one of the most expensive too.

- **EMF detector:** This piece of equipment detects fluctuations in electromagnetic fields. Investigators are of the opinion that the presence of a paranormal entity causes these fluctuations. Most of the detectors use a single-axis AC EMF, which is insufficient to detect natural sources. The latest in EMF detectors is the TriField Natural EM Meter, which detects changes in electrical or magnetic fields.

- **Carbon monoxide detector:** High levels of carbon monoxide induce dizziness and other symptoms associated with paranormal experience, even hallucinations. By measuring the amount of carbon monoxide we can rule out that the person was under its influence when he claimed to have the experience.

- **Gauss multidetector:** This device detects gauss fields on a far more sensitive level than an EMF meter.

- **REM-Pod:** This detects energy disturbances and fluctuations in a 360-degree circle.

- **Infrared motion detector:** These sensors measure people's skin temperature through the heat emitted from their body at invisible wavelengths, in contrast to background objects at room temperature.

- **Magnetic field sensor:** This high-end device can detect, monitor, and document even the slightest change in a magnetic field through computer software enhancement. The Rhode Island Paranormal Research Group & Society (TRIPRG) has used this device to successfully confirm the presence of entities when psychic investigators are trying to communicate with them. These magnetic field sensors are so sensitive they can detect even the slightest shift in the earth's gravitational fields.

- **Digital thermo-hygrometer:** This is an invaluable tool to record temperature and humidity data. Investigators say it is worth its weight in gold, particularly when investigating orb activity and determining whether an orb is natural or paranormal.

- **Ovilus and Frank's Box/ghost box:** These devices analyze and make sense of recorded speech (more on this later in the chapter).

- **Sound level meter:** This device measures the types of sounds you hear.
- **Jacob's ladder:** This is a potentially dangerous tool made of two parallel pieces of wire with a continuous path of electrical current between them. As electricity moves up the wires, they form an arc at the top.
- **Laptop computer:** Use a computer of your choice for recording data.
- **Mini-strobe light:** A strobe light can help make quick movements by a spirit seem slower.
- **Facial composite software program:** This type of software could help you identify faces you find in photos or on video.

Should you decide to shop online, check out www.ghosthunterstore.net.

SOLAR ACTIVITY AFFECTS ELECTRONICS

Many paranormal researchers believe that solar activity has an effect on electronic equipment and ghosts themselves. Geomagnetic field disturbances may damage power systems, cause false readings, or give a boost of energy to spirit manifestations and interactions.

Following is more information about infrared motion sensors and EMF detectors, as well as information about thermometers and ELF meters. Of the more advanced tools, these are some of the most popular and easy-to-use options.

THERMOMETERS

Sensing cold spots and recording sudden temperature fluctuations is an important part of ghost hunting and is of major interest to investigators. One hypothesis is that when there is a sudden drop in temperature in a given area, something is drawing energy in an attempt to manifest.

INFRARED MOTION DETECTORS

Easily available and cheaply purchased, these instruments can detect anomalies in a controlled area in two ways:

1. The device's passive infrared motion detector sweeps the zone and compares the area's thermal makeup to the reading it took upon activation.
2. The device detects noise in the sweep area and any sudden disturbance in the room's air mass. Small objects, even on the molecular level, will displace enough air within the room to trip a warning signal.

EMF AND ELF METERS

Although skeptics say EMF (electromagnetic field) and ELF (extremely low frequency) meters are useless because they pick up so many signals from the environment, these devices are widely used by ghost hunters who allege they are very helpful in detecting paranormal activity. However, these meters all require a certain amount of familiarization and training. Remember that any electrical equipment, no matter what model or brand, can give a false reading in the presence of any of the following:

- Poorly grounded or unshielded structural wiring
- Microwave ovens in use
- Dimmer switches
- Cellular phones in use
- FM, FRS, GMRS, and CB radio transceivers in use
- Air conditioning and power system/stations
- Television screens, plasma screens, and LCD screens
- Computers
- Power lines within 100 yards, especially high-voltage (tension) towers and transformers
- Fuse boxes

Any of these can cause false positives, so it's best to reserve your equipment for use at sites that are off the grid and have no nearby power source.

MESSAGES FROM THE OTHER SIDE

Ghostly images, faces, and even hands have appeared on television screens over the years—when the television sets are turned off. In one instance, the face of Prince Albert, who died in 1861, appeared on the screen of an unplugged television set. Some people have reported their television sets turning on in the middle of the night, with strange smoky shapes swirling across the screen.

Recording Your Findings

Whether you're working alone or with a group, with high-tech equipment or pencil and paper, you'll need to record what you experience so you can review it later. Proper documentation of these events is necessary, not only to ensure credibility but also to aid in subsequent investigations. With the use of certain techniques, it is possible to record your findings so that these phenomena can be explained.

STEPS TO RECORD PERSONAL FINDINGS

Record what happens as soon as possible after the experience so that the event is still fresh in your memory. Write down the following details:

- **Location:** Write down the exact location of where you were when you had the experience. Was it in your home? If so, in which room? Was it outside? Where exactly? Be very specific.

- **State:** What state were you in? Were you sitting, standing, lying down, facing something or someone? Had you taken any kind of drugs or stimulants, or had you been drinking? Were there other people with you? Were you tired, sleepy, or wide awake? Were you excited? Had you just read a book on this topic or been with someone who had narrated a similar experience? Anything at all that might have contributed to or induced the experience must be noted.

- **Environmental conditions:** Record whether it was night or day, bright or gloomy. If it was night, was the lighting adequate, or were there dark shadows? Was it a full moon or no moon?

- **Description of the phenomenon:** If it was something you saw, describe it objectively. Write down its shape, color, the clothes it was wearing, its size, etc. If it was something you felt, then describe the feeling in detail.

- **Proximity:** How close were you to the phenomenon? Try to give as accurate an estimation as possible.

- **Action:** If it was something you saw, record what it did. Were its arms raised? Did it move? Did it make any noises? Try to remember and record as much detail as possible.

- **Timing:** Be sure to record the duration of the experience. (Write down the starting and ending times.)

- **Submit report:** Hand over your report to a legitimate paranormal research group in your area or a nationally recognized organization. Ask other witnesses to sign the report to provide authenticity.

To add weight to your recordings, write down your personal details, such as name, address, age, gender, and any other relevant information. Make a drawing of the area and of what you saw. In some cases, these drawings are very helpful. Take a picture of the phenomenon. Many times people forget to capture the phenomenon even though they have a camera. Photos lend greater authenticity to your statement.

Studying the Experiences of Others

Besides these firsthand experiments, you can also carry out studies of phenomena experienced by others. Sometimes you can make connections or come up with theories that others haven't seen. Prominent phenomena that directly act as evidence of the existence of afterlife include:

- Xenoglossy, where a person is able to speak or write in a particular language without ever having learned it or having been exposed to it
- Viewings of apparitions and other signs of the presence of a dead person
- Near-death experiences, where a person comes back from the dead and has a vivid memory of that experience
- Spontaneous recall of past life, where a person starts narrating accurate facts, including places and names, about her past life

STEPS TO RECORD OTHER PEOPLE'S FINDINGS

According to Richard Southall, author of *How to Be a Ghost Hunter*, you should follow a four-step approach.

1. **Interview the eyewitness(es):** When a sighting is reported, the person(s) who saw or felt the phenomenon must be interviewed. His body language must be noted while recounting the experience.

2. **Research relevant history:** Independent of the witness, the area's history regarding such occurrences must be tabulated.

3. **Investigate the area:** This includes photographing the area, determining the right time to investigate, and following up on every lead to the phenomenon.

4. **Draw conclusions:** From the recorded data, conclude the investigation by citing what the experience is likely to be.

When carrying out studies of secondhand experiences, make sure that you record all the facts correctly. Carefully interview those who witnessed the phenomenon and the person who experienced it. Be rigorous in your research so that it can stand up to the scrutiny of a skeptic. Always remember that just as there are many believers in the afterlife, there are also many critics, and to be able to convince them, you need evidence that can withstand a scientific trial.

Instrumental Transcommunication (ITC)

An exciting more recent development in paranormal investigating is the ability to have actual conversations with the dead using new and improved technology.

THE OVILUS AND THE GHOST BOX

The controversial Ovilus is a speech-synthesis device that is currently enjoying great popularity. The device came into widespread use after being featured on several paranormal television programs, such as *Ghost Adventures* and *Paranormal State*.

The Ovilus's electronic sensors detect electromagnetic field changes. These changes combine with other data to generate a number that correlates with an internal database of words. Then the device "utters" the words generated from that input. While in phonetic mode, the Ovilus can respond to EMF variations and form spoken words that are not contained in the device's database. This is an important function.

Investigators using the Ovilus can hear actual, audible responses to their questions, and if the responses clearly relate to the investigation, it can be a very validating experience.

There are many types of these devices, including the Ovilus 5, Paranormal Puck 2, Video Ovilus, the PX, and the Talker. Later models have bigger databases to draw from and offer more features. They all have built-in EMF meters, and some have several LEDs that indicate EMF levels in the vicinity. Look for a model that has several LEDs that indicate the EMF levels in the room.

SKEPTICISM

Groups that follow a strictly scientific approach to investigations often choose *not* to use the Ovilus, stating that it produces results that are random and cannot be verified. Additionally, they are open to broad interpretation by credulous investigators/ghost hunters.

One such group is Scientific Paranormal Investigative Research Information and Technology (S.P.I.R.I.T.), directed by David Rountree. Rountree, an audio engineer, is an expert on electronic voice phenomena (EVPs). He believes the evidence he has collected indicates the phenomena derive from an EMF in the audio spectrum.

Despite some skeptics, the Ovilus is a very intriguing addition to the investigator's toolkit.

FRANK'S BOX (A.K.A. GHOST BOX)

This device is similar to the Ovilus. Created by Frank Sumption in 2002, Frank's Box scans AM frequencies up and down the radio dial in order to create white noise. It is noisy and somewhat annoying when in operation. Though not designed with paranormal investigating in mind (apparently the inventor felt the results were too open to interpretation), many groups are fascinated by the results they are getting. If you'd rather take the DIY approach, there are plans on the Internet that allow handy folks to build their own ghost boxes.

Miscellaneous Equipment

These items are not necessarily widely used in the field by all investigators, but depending on your interest level, budget, and goals, they might be right for you.

AIR ION COUNTER

The air ion counter is used for the detection of both positive and negative natural and artificial ions. It is standard paranormal theory that when a ghost/spirit is about to manifest, a certain amount of energy is drawn from the surrounding environment or from nearby sources. This meter measures the resulting change in the positive or negative ions (electrostatic energy) in the air. It is a fascinating tool in the paranormal investigator's arsenal that has the following features:

- Audible notification of activity
- Visual notification of activity
- Long battery life (up to eighteen hours of continuous use on a single battery)
- Telescopic antennae for maximum signal gain

GEIGER COUNTER

Some ghost hunters say that if you're serious about your research, this sort of meter (most often associated with radiation) may be a good choice. These meters are tough, durable, portable, and powerful. They're also very affordable. The theory is that paranormal energy ionizes the air, and this meter detects that change instantly. It is a simple instrument with a special Geiger-Muller tube detector that senses changes in the number of negatively and positively charged ions on site at investigations.

BLACK LIGHT

Inexpensive and portable, a black light, or UV light, is an interesting multiuse tool for investigators. It can be used to detect airborne particles in a room or building, and it also helps investigators to distinguish between true orb phenomena and nonparanormal airborne contaminants.

GEAR AND WEATHER-APPROPRIATE CLOTHING

Most ghost hunters in northern regions talk about the benefits of layering and wearing thermal underwear on hunts during the colder months. It is important to be practical. Investigators who are out late at night in dark areas are quite often without heat of any kind. Comfort and protection from the elements become very big priorities during overnight hunts. Comfortable shoes or sneakers are a must too.

Make sure you have clothing with lots of deep pockets to stash your ghost hunting paraphernalia. Many researchers wear fishing vests, but now you can actually find online stores that sell clothing designed for ghost hunters. Thermal blankets should be kept on hand, and thermal packs that can be slipped into pockets and gloves are extremely helpful.

OTHER USES FOR BLACK LIGHTS

Some paranormal investigators theorize that you can use a black light to "push" spirits out of an area and herd them toward another space, where they can then perhaps be photographed or contacted. Many of these very affordable devices also come with a flashlight feature.

Tips for Investigators

Ken DeCosta, the founder/director/chief investigator of RISEUP Paranormal, a nonprofit organization that specializes in the investigation of paranormal activity within the realms of hauntings, UFO experiences, and cryptozoology, has some important tips to share with investigators. For example, "The functions and purposes of equipment used on investigations these days are typically misunderstood. EMF meters do not detect the presence of spirits, despite insistence to the contrary."

USING EMF METERS SCIENTIFICALLY

RISEUP Paranormal notes that EMF meter usage "should be limited to determining manmade sources of EMF fields and used in conjunction with a TriField Natural EM Meter set to 'RF' (radio frequency) to discern microwave signals from anything anomalous. If an unusual response comes from an EMF meter where there are no fields obviously present, the potential effects should be corroborated with other equipment at your disposal to see whether they are affected as well."

CAMERA AND RECORDER PLACEMENT

RISEUP Paranormal explains, "Cameras and recorders should not be placed anywhere near where an EMF is detected, as it can interfere with the equipment's basic functions. Whether normal-level EMF found in typical household environments affects humans adversely is inconclusive. Stationary IR cameras are normally not used to catch ghostly activity, but to monitor the area and give us an idea where everyone is at all times, to eliminate any false positives. Doorways should be in the shot if at all possible. It is extremely rare when any spirit activity is caught on camera. Handheld video cameras are used to follow the investigators through the location for the same reason."

RECORDER-SPECIFIC TIPS

RISEUP Paranormal says, "Digital recorders are very useful in our investigations, but they should be shielded (metal casing) and never held in hand as any rubbing against the microphone can be interpreted as something other than natural. External microphones should be used to eliminate any internal recorder noise from creating a false positive. Recorders should reproduce all frequencies between 30 Hz up to 12 kHz at a minimum. This should be listed in their specifications. It should record in stereo and have a USB port to download files to a PC or laptop. MP3 is not a good format to record in, as you will lose some of the clarity of the recording. A good technique we use is the placement of microphones throughout a location in order to monitor sounds remotely. In this scenario, no investigators are present and the location simply 'speaks' to us without human interaction. A sound program like Audacity or Adobe Audition can be loaded onto a laptop for real-time listening via headphones at another area of the location."

PART 3

Near-Death Experiences and Miracles

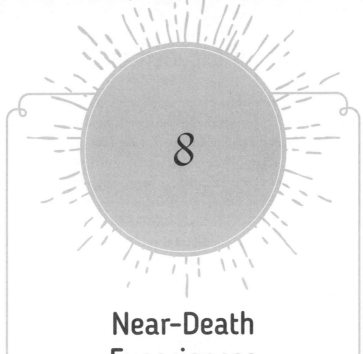

Near-Death Experiences

Have you ever thought of your own death—what actually happens when your body shuts down? Some people have experienced an event that is so close to death that it could be that glimpse into the afterlife that people have searched for since the beginning of time. Research and studies have shown that these near-death experiences (NDEs) can be so overwhelming that they leave an everlasting impression on the subject that changes his outlook on life forever.

Near-Death Experiences, Defined

Throughout the ages there have been numerous reports of phenomena surrounding people who have briefly died and come back to share experiences of an afterlife. From the ancient Greeks to modern-day people around the world, history is filled with stories of encounters with the other side. Many experiences were thought to be specific to various religions or cultures, but with time and the advancement of technology, these experiences are now being investigated and discussed openly throughout the world.

Dr. Raymond Moody coined the term *near-death experience (NDE)* in his 1975 bestselling book, *Life After Life*. Dr. Moody investigated hundreds of cases of people who were clinically dead and brought back to life to report similar extraordinary experiences from the other side.

There are many similarities in NDEs among people who have experienced them. Common phenomena (discussed later in the chapter) include:

- The feeling of being outside of the body
- The sensation of entering a tunnel
- The presence of a strong, white light
- Encountering deceased loved ones
- Experiencing a series of powerful memories from throughout their lives

---

HOW MANY PEOPLE HAVE HAD NDEs?

According to a Gallup poll, approximately 8 million Americans claim to have had a near-death experience. Many have reprioritized their lives after the experience.

Many people who have a near-death experience return with a new outlook on life that is based on universal values and a deeper sense of spirituality. Whatever their prior beliefs, they often feel a greater appreciation for life itself and a renewed sense of purpose. Their priorities may shift toward more compassionate interactions with others and increased focus on current relationships.

MESSAGES FROM THE OTHER SIDE

Here's a first-person account of an NDE:

While out fishing one day my boat started to take on water so I called for help, but just before they arrived a wave capsized my craft and I went into the water. I tried to swim to the rescue boat but I started to swallow a lot of water. The next thing I knew I was in the ER looking at the doctors as they were working on me. All of a sudden I felt like I was going to faint, and then I was out cold. The next thing I knew I seemed to be up near the ceiling of an operating room looking down at myself. There was a lot of commotion going on and I heard a nurse say, "We lost him." The doctor said, "We only have a short time." They all were trying to revive me. I was then in this dark tunnel. The tunnel seemed to be made of rings, and I felt like I was being pulled through it. I saw a bright light and I remember seeing my father and a few other people whom I knew. There were others there too. Some I did not recognize, but I felt like they were not strangers but people who I felt comfortable with.

I was told I had to return to finish my learning. I was surrounded by overwhelming joy and comfort until I felt snapped back into my physical body. The doctor said, "Welcome home." I was too weak to tell him that I had felt at home on the other side.

Science and NDEs

Not very long ago, when people encountered sudden medical emergencies that brought them to the precipice of death, there was often nothing that could be done for them and they naturally died. With the advent of modern medical devices, many individuals who have been face-to-face with their own demise have experienced a reversal of the dying process at the very time of their transition. Medical personnel who have witnessed the NDE phenomena and researchers who are interested in NDEs have begun a vast number of studies in search of the explanation for these events.

NDEs IN DIFFERENT CULTURES

Near-death experiences have been reported in all religions and cultures. These events have not been selectively associated with adults only, as many children have also experienced these episodes. The fact that some children have recounted similar experiences without having a lifetime of religious and cultural attachments is very intriguing and has been the focus of some investigations.

Some scientists have theorized that the NDE phenomena are caused by biological conditions occurring during the time of death. For example, the optic nerve could be affected, thus causing the tunnel-like experiences. The lack of oxygen to the brain has also been thought to cause some of the phenomena.

However, some of these theories have produced more questions than answers. If an NDE were a totally natural biological event, then why wouldn't every patient who experiences cardiac arrest have one? If patients were clinically dead, how would they remember the event in vivid detail? How can children describe meeting deceased relatives they never met or even knew about before the NDE?

Dr. Pim van Lommel, when referencing a study conducted in the Netherlands, said, "In our study 282 patients (82 percent) did not have any memory of the period of unconsciousness, 62 patients (18 percent) however reported a NDE with all the 'classical' elements. Between the two groups there was no difference in the duration of cardiac arrest or unconsciousness, intubation, medication, fear of death before cardiac arrest, gender, religion, education or foreknowledge about NDE."

Clinical Death versus Conscious Death

The idea of "death" has many forms, definitions, and philosophical implications. Death seems relatively easy to determine. If the body does not respond to stimuli, is immobile, and shows no sign of breathing or a heartbeat, the person is considered dead, right?

However, as medical education advanced, new possibilities began to form concerning when and how a person had achieved her biological end. With the use of ventilators and other medical apparatus, it was not always apparent when the real end of consciousness had occurred because machines could be used to continue the breathing process and assist the heart.

In 1968 a Harvard Medical School committee determined the benchmark for declaring the legal death of a human: "whole brain death." The Uniform Determination of Death Act, passed in 1981, provides the legal definition of death as either "irreversible cessation of circulatory or respiratory functions" or "irreversible cessation of all functions of the brain, including the brainstem." Brain death is considered legal death in the United States and throughout most of the world.

THE MYSTERIES OF BRAIN DEATH

Some scientists have theorized that NDEs could be caused by clinical death of the brain. However, evidence that people return to consciousness with previously unknown knowledge, and that some are given the choice to stay on the earth while others are not, challenges the assumption that all brains die basically in the same biological way.

Conscious death, the ability to lose self-awareness of being and connection to the environment, is much more difficult to define. Some scientists associate conscious death with clinical death, while others separate it into its own category of study. Philosophers are probably better suited to answer this question, but modern technology does shed some light on the possibilities.

The question of clinical death versus conscious death might be like comparing apples to oranges. Clinical death is based on a physical determination of events on a biological physical being, while conscious death might be an invalid term altogether. Scientific studies on near-death events, out-of-body experiences, and quantum physics open the door to the possibility of consciousness surviving after the declaration of clinical death.

Ongoing studies of consciousness suggest that it might be separate from the physical body but have an interaction with the living tissue of the brain. This brings up the dilemma of the real human essence. Is a human just a chemical and biological physical structure—the body—or a spirit consciousness? Someday, it may be shown that perhaps the physical body houses the spirit consciousness.

Common Feelings, Sensations, and Sights

What makes near-death experiences so interesting to researchers is the fact that so many of the people who have experienced them report common elements. Religious and cultural backgrounds do not seem to alter the main characteristics of the experiences. Ruling out these possibilities as the cause of the phenomena can help researchers focus on other areas of study, such as the mind-body connection.

THE OUT-OF-BODY EXPERIENCE

A common sensation of an NDE is the feeling of leaving the physical body and floating free of the confines of the physical world. This is the point where the individual realizes that something extraordinary is happening to him and he begins to observe his altered surroundings. A person having an out-of-body experience sees himself along with the surroundings, often from "above." People have reported the exact movements and conversations of medical personnel in the emergency room after being declared clinically dead.

THE SILVER CORD

The silver cord has been described as a thin iridescent light membrane that connects an individual to the physical body during an out-of-body event. People who have experienced this phenomenon often report thinking that if the cord were severed, they would continue on to the afterlife and not have the ability to return to the physical world.

THE TUNNEL AND LIGHT

After an NDE, many people talk about seeing a tunnel, often with a light at the end of it. People report feeling drawn to the tunnel by an outside force, and upon entering it, feeling as if they are being propelled through it at a high rate of speed. NDE subjects commonly describe a slim glimmer of light at the end that brightens to an extreme degree and becomes what has been described as a living entity of light.

CONCEPT OF TIME

NDE subjects report an altered perception of time during the experience. An event that actually lasts a few minutes can seem to go on for hours or days. People also remember feeling as if time does not exist. There seems to be no beginning or end to this new existence they are experiencing.

KNOWLEDGE

The knowledge that is transferred during the NDE does not seem to be a surprise to many, as they remember the essence of the discussions and the meaning, but not always the details. They remember that it all makes sense, but they are not sure how or why it makes sense. It is like having a gut feeling about something: You're not sure why you feel a certain way, but you trust yourself that it's right. When asked, "What is the most important thing in our lives?" many subjects respond with "love"—to give love, to accept love, and to learn from love.

THE LIFE REVIEW

Another common element of an NDE is called a life review. People report experiencing a review of their complete lives, often with lightning speed and clarity. Some people report a greater understanding of how their actions have affected others after undergoing a life review.

A panoramic review of an entire life seems like an overwhelming concept, but people who have gone through an NDE say that it can be a learning experience, and many people describe feeling surrounded by support and unconditional love.

The experience of a life review has been described as watching an intricately detailed movie in an instant. People say that they seemed able to relive every thought and every encounter they ever had. They also felt as if they experienced the reactions and emotions they caused in every person they ever came into contact with. This complete empathy makes people realize how influential their interactions have been for others.

People also report a sense of judgment, not by others but by themselves. Dannion Brinkley, author of the bestselling book *Saved by the Light*, said of his experiences with with panoramic review during NDEs, "You are the toughest judge you will ever have." The review seems to give individuals the opportunity to reprioritize their lives in the future. After such a profound experience, many people say they have lost their fear of death and have become more compassionate, caring individuals.

SOME NDEs ARE NOT PLEASANT

Not all reported NDEs have the traits of peace, love, and understanding. Some people report coming into contact with a dark void, lacking any compassion or light. They feel as if they're surrounded with negative energies that are filled with anger and arrogance and lacking the concept of love.

Some people say that they were given the choice to stay and continue their existence or pass to the other side, while others report being told it wasn't their time, followed by a reconciliation with their physical bodies. People who have reported having the choice often say that they were torn between choosing this peaceful, loving state and returning to the physical realm in order to care for their children or other loved ones. For those whose time has not come, there seems to be unfinished business, things to be learned and experienced, for either themselves or others they might interact with at a future time.

MESSAGES FROM THE OTHER SIDE

Here's another first-person account:

I was in a dark void with nothing around me, and then I noticed a small white light that began to grow as I moved quickly toward it. The light seemed to be alive. It had an unbelievable feeling of love to it and I just smiled as it surrounded me.

My whole life was then shown to me. I saw everything I had ever done, good and bad. I wish I hadn't done some things in my past but I had a feeling that it was all right.

Everything happened so fast. I asked questions and knew the answers at almost the same time I asked them. I was not talking like we do but was communicating through emotion and my mind. There was an all-knowing understanding. I realized that the only thing in life is love. I have changed my life to be more kind toward others. There is definitely a God. Maybe not with a robe and beard, but love is the way to recognize him.

THE LIGHT BEING

People report coming into contact with a being of light that accompanies them during their life review. This being, which can be communicated with telepathically, is described as loving and compassionate.

ENCOUNTERING DECEASED LOVED ONES

A comforting part of some near-death experiences involves encountering deceased relatives, friends, and loved ones. People say that these entities seem to appear to help with the transition from the physical plane to the other side. Some people report the presence of other beings that are not recognized but seem to have an emotional family connection.

It's not uncommon for a person to recognize the unidentified figures once the NDE is over and the person describes it to others. Often, friends and relations can identify a relative who died without ever meeting the NDE participant. This happens often with younger children.

MESSAGES FROM THE OTHER SIDE

Here's another first-person account of an NDE:

I was on my way to work on a farm early one morning with a friend of mine. I was driving my truck about 75 mph because we were late. I started to turn the radio on and when I looked up I was leaving the road. I tried to quickly turn the steering wheel the other way but it just rolled the truck over and down an embankment.

I was thrown from the truck into a ditch. I broke a bunch of bones, cut myself up, and banged my head bad. I was out cold. My friend called for help and I was put into an ambulance.

I felt out of my body at this point. I could see the EMTs working on me, but I felt no pain. It was weird—it was like watching someone else being worked on. Then I saw a light and started to go toward it. I noticed all my relatives there, smiling at me. My uncle came up to me and said I had to go back. "It's not your time," he said.

Before I knew it, I was in the ambulance feeling like I had been hit by a house. I will always remember the loving feeling that was all around me when I was in that light. It's difficult to explain.

Many report a sense of being home. The environment sometimes appears to be a past residence. The powerful awareness of these connections is a common trait of a near-death experience.

NONFAMILY ENCOUNTERS

Those who have had a near-death experience sometimes report encountering religious figures, angels, or guides. They may feel as if they have known these entities for a lifetime or even more than one lifetime.

MESSAGES FROM THE OTHER SIDE

Here's another first-person account:

I was at the beach one afternoon and got caught in an undertow. I tried very hard to swim, but I slipped under the surface. I started to inhale water and realized I was drowning. I blanked out and began to see shadows of people I didn't know. I did not recognize them but I seemed to know they were family. How I knew this I don't know. I just knew. I began to hear this beautiful music and was moving through a tunnel toward a being of light. I knew it was God because it was surrounded with pure love. Just as I was getting close to this being I shot back into my body and I awoke lying on my side on a rescue boat. I now have no fear of dying; I know what's on the other side and it's great!

Family pets have also been observed in these surroundings. The feeling of being reunited with a well-loved and missed pet brings great joy to the owner.

People say that contact with deceased friends, work associates, and distant relatives can have a tremendous positive effect on them, even if they were never previously close. These people often provide insight into ongoing events or reassurance that a reunion with loved ones will happen at some time in the future.

TELEPATHIC COMMUNICATION

A person who has experienced an NDE often describes communication that takes place without words being spoken. Questions seem to be asked and answered through mental connections. Another commonly reported experience is a question that goes unanswered, as if it's too soon to know the answer.

A CHOICE

Some people realize that a choice is to be made concerning the future—either to join some kind of afterlife or to return to their physical body. Sometimes the individual makes this choice and at other times, it seems as if it's made for her.

Scientific Studies

There are hundreds of published research papers and scientific studies on near-death experiences, and many more studies are being conducted today throughout the world. The field of NDE investigations is growing and the mainstream scientific and medical communities are taking notice.

A CHILDREN'S STUDY

P.M.H. Atwater is one of the original researchers in the field of near-death studies. In her research, she studied more than 270 children who have had NDEs. Her findings revealed the following:

- Seventy-six percent reported a comforting "initial" experience. Such experiences involved things like a "loving nothingness," a friendly voice, a visitation by a loving being, an out-of-body experience, and/or the peacefulness of either a safe light or safe, dark place.

- Nineteen percent reported a pleasurable or heaven-like experience.

- Three percent reported a distressing or hell-like experience.

- Two percent had a "transcendent" experience in which they felt they acquired special knowledge.

The most commonly reported type of childhood NDE is the "initial" experience.

In an episode of meningitis, a six-year-old reported being out of her body with a sense of being completely free of pain and totally surrounded by love. She reported feeling like a soul—neither boy nor girl, neither grownup nor child. She felt a sense of absolute peace and completeness. When she looked down, she saw a girl lying in bed and empathized with her pain. On reflection, she realized she must be that girl, and with that thought, she was back in her body.

Children offer a unique look into NDEs as they provide a less "cluttered" view of the event. They have not been exposed to as many theories, beliefs, or life situations as adults.

THE DUTCH NDE STUDY

The Dutch author and researcher Dr. Pim van Lommel studied near-death experiences of cardiac patients for almost two decades after noticing similar experiences of patients who survived cardiac arrest.

Dr. van Lommel and colleagues began a study in 1988, which consisted of 344 survivors of cardiac arrest. This study was created to observe and record patients' experiences under controlled conditions at ten different hospitals. Similar studies were carried out in Britain and the United States, with more than 500 total participants. In 2001 this major study was published in the medical periodical *The Lancet*.

The study found that some patients experienced a form of increased consciousness after cardiac arrest, which should not be possible, as breathing and circulation of the blood to the brain have stopped. The patients recalled out-of-body experiences, meeting deceased relatives, and seeing their entire lives played out in front of them.

According to Dr. van Lommel, "several theories have been proposed to explain NDE. However, in our prospective study we did not show that psychological, physiological or pharmacological factors caused these experiences after cardiac arrest."

9

Miracles

Miracles have fascinated and comforted millions of people throughout history. There have always been conflicting views as to the origin of these events. While many religions include the belief that miracles are divine interventions, science holds that there is no phenomenon that cannot be explained, even if the technology needed to test the phenomenon does not exist at the moment. With the help of modern science, some miracles can now be examined more closely to acquire the origin of the event and to bridge the gap between religious and cultural views and the scientific community.

Visions by Multiple Witnesses

Phenomena such as visions, healings, and prophecies that fall under the heading of "miraculous" are all events that usually either transcend human powers or defy the laws of nature, as a result of the apparent intervention of divine or supernatural forces. Some consider these events to be acts of God.

An interesting observation about miraculous visions is that their "greatness" is often comparable to their number of witnesses. Individuals and smaller groups of people witness smaller miracles, and larger, more awe-inspiring miracles tend to have crowds of hundreds, even thousands, of witnesses.

VISIONS IN MEDJUGORJE

Since June 24, 1981, several people in the town of Medjugorje in Citluk, Bosnia and Herzegovina, have been seeing visions of Mother Mary, who speaks with them and guides them. Six children, Ivanka Ivankovic, Mirjana Dragicevic, Vicka Ivankovic, Ivan Dragicevic, Ivan Ivankovic, and Milka Pavlovic, saw a beautiful lady with a child in her arms at 6:00 P.M. on the Crnica Hill known as Podbrdo. She asked them to come closer, but they ran away. The next day at the same time and the same place the lady appeared again, and this time the children embraced her. Ivan Ivankovic and Milka Pavlovic were not there; in their places were Marija Pavlovic and Jakov Colo. On the third day, when the lady appeared, Mirjana asked her name, to which she replied, "I am the Blessed Virgin Mary." To this day, these children, now adults, continue to speak to and see the apparition. The vision tells them to have faith in God.

OUR LADY OF LOURDES

The shrine of Our Lady of Lourdes in France is one of the most visited shrines in the world because of the healing spring that appeared during the vision of the Blessed Virgin Mary to Bernadette Soubirous, a poor fourteen-year-old girl.

STRENGTH IN NUMBERS

When one person is witness to a type of paranormal phenomenon, she can be open to questions of personal bias, financial gain, or even seeking public attention. However, when multiple witnesses are involved, more critical attention is brought to the event, which then can be investigated without the possibility of one person's own agenda. Multiple-witness visions add a great deal of weight to the possibilities of the existence of a supernatural world interacting with this physical one.

Mother Mary appeared eighteen times to this girl, the first of which was on February 11, 1858. Bernadette saw her in the grotto of Massabielle, where she told her, "I am the Immaculate Conception." On one occasion, she asked Bernadette to wash her face in the fountain where there was no water. But when Bernadette scratched the ground, a stream of water with miraculous healing powers gushed forth. It is this stream that attracts people from the world over even to this day. Bernadette became a nun and continued to see these visions. She died when she was thirty-five.

THE FATIMA VISIONS

During World War I, on May 13, 1916, three shepherd children, Lucia dos Santos, aged nine, and her cousins Francisco and Jacinta Marto, aged eight and six respectively, saw a vision of Mother Mary at Fatima, near Lisbon in Portugal. She asked them to come there for six months on the same date. Various messages were given and people from all of Portugal began to visit the site. In October 1916, as many as 70,000 people saw the "sun dancing in the sky," and then falling to earth before ascending back toward the sky.

OUR LADY OF LIGHT, ZEITOUN, EGYPT

The apparition of what is called Our Lady of Light was seen on April 2, 1968, in Zeitoun, Egypt. This apparition was witnessed by tens of thousands of people, including Christians, Jews, Muslims, and non-believers. At first she appeared surrounded by light in a kneeling position on the roof of a church. Farouk Mohammed Atwa, a Muslim and the first man to see her, was healed from a case of gangrene. Over the next three years, Our Lady appeared repeatedly, usually around two to three times a week, mostly at night. Orbs of white light would precede her apparition, and sometimes white doves would accompany her, at times flying in a cross formation, as she walked around the dome of the church. More than 100,000 people would gather to view the events.

The Roman Catholic Church finally approved the apparition as a visitation of the Holy Mother. She apparently had a three-dimensional quality with a flesh-colored face and hands, and she would show up in the thousands of photos that were taken of her, along with the light orbs and rays.

Healings of Unknown Origin

Almost everyone has heard stories of people miraculously healed after modern medical science has given up hope of a cure. These miracle healings of unknown origin or reason have baffled humankind for centuries. Disappearing tumors, recoveries from deathbeds, and even simple healings of common ailments through prayer, healing touch, distant-healing methods, and many other such paranormal means have been cited, researched, and discussed extensively.

MIRACLE HEALING THROUGH THE AGES

Instances of miracle healings have been cited through the history of mankind, from the ancient civilizations to the modern world of today. Paracelsus, a Swiss physician and alchemist born in the fifteenth century who is often regarded as the father of modern pharmacology, is believed to have used not only physiological but also psychical methods of curing people. He believed that there exists a luminous vital force around us, which can be manipulated to heal people.

Franz Mesmer, a famous psychic healer of the eighteenth century, talked of a universal energy fluid, which could be directed to heal people. He was known for his unconventional methods of healing, which included hypnosis, healing touch, and use of magnets on his patients.

Native Americans have practiced spiritual healing for ages. Each tribe has a spiritual leader called a shaman, who is said to have healing powers. Christians strongly believe in the healing power of prayer, and many claims of faith healings from across the world are commonly heard.

VARIOUS FORMS AND TYPES
OF MIRACLE HEALINGS

Miraculous healings that cannot be attributed to natural causes are associated with paranormal methods or phenomena. In many cases, these are simply said to be the work of God. Most religious healings are said to be achieved through prayers, which in some cultures are performed according to special rituals and practices.

MIRACLES BEYOND SCIENTIFIC EXPLANATION

There have been many unexplained cases of healings not associated with medical science. Eastern medicine has utilized various alternative modalities in treatment of the ill, with positive results. Science continues to research the possibilities of healing through touch, prayer, and sound.

There are also other types of paranormal healings, which are said to result from bio-energy or life energy, which flows through all living beings. This universal vital force can be manipulated to relieve patients of their diseases or sufferings. The healing methods, which leverage this paranormal energy and phenomena, include healing touch, distant healing, and psychic surgery. Alternative healing therapies associated with this school of thought include Pranic healing and Reiki.

Besides these paranormal healing methods, some materials and astronomical bodies are also thought to have miraculous healing powers. Crystal healing is a popular curative therapy adopted by many people worldwide.

ARE PARANORMAL HEALINGS FOR REAL?

Many cases of quackery related to miracle healings have been exposed. Methods like psychic surgery have come under severe criticism after cases of serious fraud were discovered. Stephen Barrett, noted American psychiatrist and co-founder of the National Council Against Health Fraud (NCAHF), has extensively studied cases of miracle healings and found no conclusive evidence that any of the patients were healed by the psychic methods.

MESSAGES FROM THE OTHER SIDE

One story of a modern-day miracle involves the inexplicable recovery of a terminal woman after praying to Mother Mary MacKillop, an Australian nun who was declared a saint by the Catholic Church:

"The approved miracle involved the healing of a . . . woman with inoperable lung cancer during the mid 1990s. Given just a few months to live, she asked the Sisters of Joseph, which Mother Mary founded, to pray for her, and was given a relic of Mother Mary's to wear. Against all odds she not only recovered but all traces of the cancer disappeared." (Source: "The Miracles That Put Mary MacKillop on the Path to Sainthood." *Herald Sun.* December 2009.)

This was Mother Mary's second miracle and lead to her canonization by Pope Benedict XVI.

However, there are other schools of thought that try to explain otherwise. There is no doubt that some methods of psychic healings may be fraudulent, but putting all under the same category would be unfair.

Doris Kreiger, a New York University researcher, has been studying healing touch and is said to have received positive results from her study of the effect of "therapeutic touch" on hemoglobin. Sister Justice Smith, who is a biochemist, has also conducted some successful research on the effect of healing by touch on damaged and whole enzymes.

They believe that therapeutic touch, even though unexplainable as an exact scientific phenomenon, leverages the power of the dynamic electromagnetic energy fields surrounding our body, mind, and soul. These multilayered energy fields connect us with the consciousness of the universe and draw the life force to induce healing in the affected bodies. These alternative therapies of so-called "unexplained" or "miraculous" healings are said to work on the principle that states, "Energy flows where attention goes!"

In the book *Spiritual Healing*, Dr. Daniel J. Benor reports on 124 scientific studies that validate the success of various alternative healing methods. Many of the controlled studies were conducted at leading hospitals and research facilities. Therapeutic touch, Reiki, and other hands-on healing techniques are currently being used in hospitals and other treatment facilities throughout the world to reduce pain and decrease postoperative recovery times. What at one time may have been seen as miraculous may now be viewed as a new paradigm in healing.

Physical Manifestations

There have been many instances of physical manifestations of God, angels, saints, and departed souls throughout human history. Such instances have been reported across the world and have strengthened the faith of not only those who witnessed them but also those who heard or read about them.

Miracles can be defined as physical events that defy the laws of nature. Most miracles show some sort of physical manifestation that is evident not only to the individuals involved but also to the people around them. According to Reverend James Wiseman, emeritus professor of spirituality at the Catholic University of America, there are always going to be those "who see immediately the hand of God in every coincidence, and those who are going to be skeptical of everything. And there is a great in-between."

Physical manifestations surrounding miracles form an integral part of all religions, and an endless number of devotees celebrate these miracles as God's intervention in human lives. Both the Old and New Testaments of the Bible as well as the Koran are filled with accounts of miracles and wonders performed by God, angels, prophets, and saints.

DIVINE PHYSICAL MANIFESTATIONS

In 1531, Juan Diego, who had recently been converted to Christianity, saw the Virgin Mary five times in Guadalupe, Mexico. The Virgin Mary left her imprint on Juan Diego's cloak. Benoîte Rencurel, a shepherdess from Saint-Étienne-le-Laus, France, started seeing the Virgin Mary in 1664 and continued to see her throughout her life. In 1830, Catherine Labouré of France saw the Virgin Mary three times and was told to have the medal of the Immaculate Conception made to spread faith in the world. In 1846, in La Salette-Fallavaux, France, Maximin

Giraud and Mélanie Calvat saw the Virgin Mary. The Blessed Mother appeared in tears and called for penance.

In 1879, the figures of Joseph, Mary, John the Apostle, and a lamb appeared over the gable of a chapel in an Irish village. Fifteen people saw the figures, which were surrounded by a bright light. In 1932, Mary came to five children in a convent in Beauraing, Belgium, calling for the conversion of sinners and identifying herself as the "Immaculate Virgin." In 1933, Mariette Beco of Belgium saw the Virgin Mary eight times in a garden, where she identified herself as the "Virgin of the Poor." In 1981, six girls and one boy saw both Jesus and the Virgin Mary in Kibeho, Rwanda. The apparitions continued for several years and were last seen in 1989.

PHYSICAL MANIFESTATIONS OF DEPARTED SOULS

Seeing or interacting with apparitions of the deceased is a very common phenomenon. After-death communication, both natural and induced, has been extensively recorded and studied. Children who die young are often seen as apparitions by loved ones after their death. People on their deathbeds also see apparitions of deceased relatives, symbolizing their getting closer to the otherworld.

Researchers investigating these physical manifestations of the deceased have found most of the subjects to be in perfectly normal, nonhallucinatory states. In addition, some of the sightings have even yielded tangible evidence, such as broken things, a signature or words written by the apparition, and recordings on tape. Some apparitions are seen by multiple people (including the apparitions at Gettysburg

Battlefield, as previously described). This lends more credibility to the claims. Many of the sightings are unexplainable according to the natural world as we perceive it. These manifestations play an important role in strengthening faith and helping connect to what is beyond this material world.

According to Jon Butler, a Yale University professor of American history who specializes in American religion, "Most miracles have some physical manifestation that is evident not only to the individuals involved, but may be evident to the people around them. The catch is, how do you explain it?"

Unexplained Evidence

Miracles are events that are beyond the explanation of the "natural" state of affairs or science of today. They are events that stir the soul and are often thought to be works of God. There is also another school of thought that connects miracles to metaphysics, and states that miracles are projections of our own souls in an attempt to connect with our self-consciousness. This is probably the reason why many miracles are cited by the observers in times of fear, death, or some other kind of unusual circumstance.

Science can neither prove nor disprove miracles—if it can, then the event can no longer be called a miracle. People all around the world observe miracles, and their experience results in a strengthening of their belief in the existence of powers beyond the understanding of the human mind and current science.

Depending on the evidence, miracles can be broadly classified into four categories:

- **Miraculous relics:** These are usually relics of religious significance that display unexplained phenomena, like blood tears on a statue of the Virgin Mary and the Shroud of Turin.
- **Miraculous images:** These are unexplained images usually of divine nature that are spotted in unexpected places, like a religious symbol appearing on some usual object.
- **Divine experiences:** These are experiences that humans go through but are unexplainable by natural laws. This includes experiences such as prophesying, imperviousness to poisons, and speaking in tongues.
- **Faith healing:** The evidence in these miracles is unexplained healing of individuals from incurable conditions or diseases, or healing of the body miraculously, without any intervention of medical science.

WELL-KNOWN CASES OF UNEXPLAINED EVIDENCE AND MIRACLES

Here's a short list of miracles, which after years of investigation and study, have remained unexplainable.

Weeping and Bleeding Statues of Religious Icons
A number of cases of statues weeping (in many cases blood tears) have occurred around the world. Famous instances of this include the

case of the Weeping Madonna of Toronto, the Jesus painting in the Bethlehem Church of the Nativity, and the statue of Christ weeping olive oil in the Antiochian Orthodox Church in Sydney. Though these incidents are often claimed to be fraudulent, several investigations and tests have yielded inconclusive evidence.

THE UNEXPLAINABLE

There are many instances of paranormal miraculous events that have been explained by science. However, there still remains the fact that science might not have the current means to explain all of these occurrences. Until they are completely explained without a doubt, they will remain miracles.

Crystal Tears of a Lebanese Girl

A Lebanese girl, Hasnah Mohamed Meselmani, produces crystal tears from her eyes. These crystals are as sharp as cut glass, but Hasnah says that she feels no pain when they are produced. These tears are produced as often as seven times a day and have been examined by medical experts, who are unable to find the reason for their occurrence.

Stigmata

Another Christian miracle, which has been reported by people from across the world, is stigmata. Afflicted people receive crucifixion and lashing wounds on their hands, feet, head, and other parts of the body, similar to those Jesus endured. These wounds are sometimes visible and accompanied by blood, while in other cases the wounds are invisible. They are almost always accompanied by pain and can last for long periods of time.

Francesco Forgione, later known as Padre Pio, was an Italian Roman Catholic priest who became famous for his stigmata. He also manifested various spiritual gifts, including the gifts of healing, bilocation, prophecy, miracles, the ability to read hearts, and extraordinary abstinence from both sleep and nourishment. He was granted sainthood after so many miracles were attributed to him.

MESSAGES FROM THE OTHER SIDE

In May 2008, a strange case of twenty-five children miraculously being healed of life-threatening conditions such as cancer and heart defects in Sacred Heart Hospital in Caracas, Venezuela, came to light. Many staffers and doctors at the hospital claimed to have seen the spirit of a doctor tending to the ailing children and then vanishing into thin air.

These and many more instances of unexplained evidence of miracles have been reported from around the world, with scientists and investigators struggling to come up with "reasonable" explanations for these happenings. Whether these are divine interventions from God or something supernatural and beyond understanding, they clearly highlight how little is known of the world and its wonders.

Science and Miracle Phenomena

The term *miracle* comes from the Latin word *mirus*, meaning "wonderful." Religious definitions usually refer to a miracle as an unexpected event attributed to divine intervention. Christian Science refers to "a divinely natural phenomenon experienced humanly as the fulfillment of spiritual law." The rise of the New Age movement has shown an increase in paranormal and religious events, such as faith healing, divine apparitions, and magical images. However, scientists consider these to be unique natural occurrences, and deny the possibility of any kind of miracle.

WHY SCIENCE IS SKEPTICAL OF MIRACLES

Throughout history, events that were once thought to be miracles have become known simply as rare occurrences with logical, scientific explanations. Examples of these kinds of "miracles" include people being struck by lightning and the birth of rare animals, such as a white buffalo or red heifer (having obviously genetic causes).

KEEP AN OPEN MIND

It is important to keep an open mind when investigating any miracle phenomenon and it should not be looked upon with bias or preconceived notions. Following the right scientific protocol in the research of the event is the best way of explaining the phenomenon.

In scientific analysis, phenomena are compared with other similar events so that the mechanisms that made them possible can be understood. Two of the fundamental issues with miracle phenomena are that they are sometimes found to be elaborate hoaxes or they are singular in their occurrence and unable to be compared for analysis.

Also, because a miracle is by definition unexplainable by the laws of nature, a lot of scientists throw out the possibility that a miracle can even exist. The other major issue with miracle claims is in their religious associations, because scientific analysis requires separating the miracle from its apparent divine creation as well as its supposed support of religiously interpreted "meaning."

Science is an ever-evolving field; thus, it may or may not be able to explain all the natural events and occurrences that take place worldwide. But once scientists and researchers find the proper tools to analyze any such event, it ceases to be a miracle. So for scientists, everything that happens in this world, however incredible it might seem, has an explanation and therefore cannot be referred to as a miracle.

HOW RELIGIONS DEFINE MIRACLES

Because of past hoaxes created to give credibility to religions, sects, or individuals seeking to influence others, the religious definition of a miracle requires that certain criteria be met. Often, so-called miracles have later been revealed to be previously misunderstood scientific phenomena due to either their infrequency or a lack of knowledge.

In light of this, some religious authorities, such as the Vatican, restrict the labeling of an event as a miracle to those complex instances that defy all natural laws and have direct religious association as proof of God's omnipotence.

The Vatican has access to a pool of sixty-plus doctors covering all the medical branches for the purpose of deciding whether any modern-day medical healing can be considered a miracle. Two specialists are assigned to each possible miracle healing to study the event. All scientific causes must be ruled out in order for the event to continue its course of examination toward being designated a miracle.

LOURDES

The Vatican established a medical bureau at Lourdes, France, to establish the authenticity of miracle healings after the apparition of Virgin Mary in 1858. It is said that Our Lady of Lourdes described a spring to Bernadette Soubirous, and it has been associated with more than 7,000 miracles. The Church takes a very strict scientific approach to the verification of such reports and therefore shares some common ground with the scientific community.

THE SEARCH WILL CONTINUE

There are very large gaps in our knowledge regarding supernatural phenomena, especially when it comes to rare occurrences. Many things that were said to be impossible at one point were later proved to be possible, such as flight, breaking the sound barrier, space travel, relativity, and quantum theory.

The intellectual struggle and the resentment it sometimes breeds between people who want to hold true to the belief in miracles and those who want to exercise scientific integrity is unnecessary. In modern-day miracle investigation, both science and religion use the same current knowledge available to try to explain phenomena that baffle the world.

MESSAGES FROM THE OTHER SIDE

A great number of modern miracles are medical in nature. In 2001, merely days after his birth, a child was diagnosed with liver failure so severe he required a liver transplant. When the initial donor liver proved incompatible, physicians were certain the baby would pass away. The events that followed astounded doctors and defied medical science:

The child's family prayed to Father George Preca, who was the first Maltese Catholic saint and creator of the Society of Christian Doctrine in Malta. They prayed that he would ask God to spare the life of their child. A glove used during the exhumation of the priest in 2000 also was placed upon the infant's body. Less than a week later, the baby's liver started to function normally, and within another four days the baby no longer required a transplant.

Source: Caldwell, Simon. "Surgeon Tells of Healed Baby, Crucial Miracle for Malta's First Saint." *Catholic News Service.* May 2007.

Appendix

Spectral Sites

Upon a first or even a second glance, a quaint farmhouse or a cornfield may seem completely ordinary. Nothing strikes the casual observer as remotely strange. But ghost hunters and psychic investigators who know the history of picturesque antebellum mansions or Civil War battlefields know differently. If ghosts are the spirits of the dead that are emotionally connected to a particular locality, and if the act of passing over was violent or accidental, the chances that the spirit of the departed will linger in some form are much stronger. Obviously, the older the property, the greater the likelihood that ghostly remnants may linger there.

Battlefields and Historic Sites

It's not surprising that many battlefields are believed to be haunted. The trauma and pain associated with such sites may linger as psychic echoes throughout eternity. Battlefields are notorious for paranormal phenomena.

GETTYSBURG

Gettysburg, Pennsylvania, is reputed to be one of the most haunted places in America—and with very good reason. From July 1 through 3, 1863, Union and Confederate forces fought each other in one of the most ferocious battles of the Civil War.

As the battle raged, Confederate sharpshooters took aim from the attic of a rambling farmhouse on the outskirts of town. Today, the Historic Farnsworth House Inn is a bed and breakfast where guests can study the bullet holes that cover the south wall. On that side of the house, many guests have reported seeing an apparition of a wounded Union soldier at the end of a bed. One woman reported that her infant was lifted by unseen hands and gently placed back down in the crib. Tourists taking pictures around or in the house have been startled when the photographs show transparent figures of men wearing Civil War–era uniforms. One visitor even claimed to have seen Confederate general Robert E. Lee sitting atop his famous gray horse, Traveller.

Residents of Gettysburg mention that during strolls across the battlefield on warm summer nights, it's not unusual to encounter hot spots. It's also common to hear gunshots, screams, and bugle calls.

During the filming of the 1993 movie *Gettysburg*, Civil War re-enactors were recruited as extras. While in uniform, one group of men found themselves confronted by a haggard old man, dressed as a Union private. The man smelled strongly of sulfur, a key ingredient of the black gunpowder used in 1863. He handed them a few musket rounds and said, "Rough one today, eh, boys?" Then he turned and walked away into the shrubbery. When the re-enactors brought the rounds into town, local experts authenticated them as original rounds, dating back to the Civil War era.

OLD GREEN EYES

Like Gettysburg, Chickamauga, Georgia, is haunted by the spirits of Civil War soldiers, but this battlefield is unique in that it is haunted by an entity that does not really fit the definition of a ghost. Known as Old Green Eyes, this entity is described as a large creature with fanglike teeth, a hairy body, and burning green eyes. The figure walks on two legs and perhaps wears a cloak. Over the years, thousands have claimed they have seen him prowling about at dusk. Some say the first sighting pre-dates or dates back to the time of the Battle of Chickamauga, which took place in September 1863.

A number of stories about the origin of Old Green Eyes have been put forth over the decades. The most common is a Native American legend about such a creature that roamed the area long ago, scavenging through the Indian villages—a description that sounds remarkably like a Sasquatch.

According to some legends, both Confederate and Union soldiers actually saw the creature creeping through the area just after the battle, carrying away dead bodies. Others claim that Old Green Eyes is the ghost of a soldier whose head was blown off by a cannon and whose body was destroyed. According to this legend, the soldier's head drifts about the battlefield, searching for its body.

FORT FEAR

Dale Kaczmarek, the director of the Ghost Research Society (GRS), claims there are more than 100 haunted hot spots in the greater Chicago area. The GRS and independent psychic investigators of Chicago know their city is home to just about every kind of apparition and phenomenon imaginable, from sightings of ghost ships on Lake Michigan to singing entities.

One of the most famous "haunt spots" is a Chicago landmark, Fort Sheridan, located north of the city and known to the locals as Fort Fear. Built along an Indian trail connecting it to Green Bay, Wisconsin, Fort Sheridan was originally a French trading post and mission established around 1670.

By the early twentieth century, the fort was all but abandoned and had fallen into disrepair. But for many years afterward, sightings of a lady in an orange dress were reported. Seen during random sunrises around the former officers' mess hall, the lady was rumored to resemble Mamie Eisenhower.

THE ROSEWELL GHOST

Elizabeth Bissette, a writer, musician, and reluctant psychic, found herself walking through the echoes of a long-gone American family when she visited the Rosewell estate in Gloucester County, Virginia. Constructed in 1725 by Mann Page, Rosewell was the ancestral home of the Page family for more than 100 years. John Page, grandson of the builder, was a schoolmate of Thomas Jefferson. In 1916, a fire swept through the mansion, gutting it and leaving only a magnificent shell, which remained a haunting testament to eighteenth-century craftsmanship and dreams.

Legends and lore associated with the estate were passed down from generation to generation, written in journals or whispered around fireplaces. Supposedly, Mann Page expired in the grand front hall of the mansion, and the bishop of Virginia proclaimed that God had struck him down for his excesses. Another rumor is that Mann died because he was cursed by the spirit of Powhatan for building the mansion on the site of Werowocomoco, the chief's village.

Tales of hauntings on the Rosewell grounds cover a broad spectrum, from full-body apparitions to moans. Vintage automobiles have even been sighted. It was this atmosphere that Elizabeth Bissette, a distant relation of the Pages, entered when she turned onto the long plantation road that led to the shell of the mansion.

Parking near the family cemetery, she and a friend wandered the grounds, taking pictures. Nothing untoward happened, except that their car stalled on their way out. "The next day," Bissette said, "I started thinking that there was a good chance the photos wouldn't turn out, because we hadn't been able to get any light." She and her friend decided to return at twilight.

"So, we got there," she continued, "and I'm taking pictures and we're standing around talking and I swear I saw behind [my companion] a man in colonial dress with his hair back in a ponytail. Young, smiling.

He winked at me and put his finger to his lips, pointing to my friend. He looked so real, I thought he was a re-enactor, that maybe they'd had an event there that day and he was messing with me and wanted to play a joke on my friend. That is, until he disappeared."

Rather than explain the inexplicable to her companion, Bissette replied jokingly that she had just seen Thomas Jefferson and that she wished he had brought his violin.

Cemeteries and Graveyards

Cemeteries and hauntings seem to go hand in hand, but in actuality, reports of haunted cemeteries are far less common than those of specter-plagued houses. However, Bachelor's Grove Cemetery in Chicago has been dubbed the most haunted cemetery in America by the GRS. The cemetery earned a frightening reputation with reports of a mysterious lady in white, flying light orbs, and even vanishing automobiles.

Located on the edge of the Rubio Woods Forest Preserve in the suburb of Midlothian, Illinois, this 200-year-old burial ground has been largely forgotten. But almost all midwestern ghost hunters place Bachelor's Grove high on their most haunted list.

Although the last actual burial in Bachelor's Grove took place in 1989, the place had been virtually abandoned and forgotten by the mid-nineteenth century. Since that time, many apparitions have been captured on film, the most famous being the image of a woman seated on a tombstone that was taken with infrared film. This spirit is known as the

White Lady or the Madonna of Bachelor's Grove. It is rumored to be the ghost of a woman buried in the cemetery next to her infant son. She has been seen on nights with a full moon, wandering about the cemetery with a baby in her arms.

RESURRECTION MARY

Resurrection Cemetery in Justice, Illinois, is haunted by an entity known as Resurrection Mary. Since the 1930s, numerous witnesses driving along Archer Avenue have reported picking up a female hitchhiker.

The young woman has blonde hair and blue eyes and is wearing a white party dress. Some of the drivers describe her as wearing a thin shawl and holding a small clutch purse. When the driver gets close to the Resurrection Cemetery gates, the woman asks to be let out, whereupon she disappears or floats through the bars of the gates. The bars bear strange handprints seared into the metal—the mark of Resurrection Mary.

Chicago area ghost hunter Richard T. Crowe claimed to have collected three dozen substantiated reports of Mary from the 1930s through the 1980s.

Schools and Churches

Illinois College was founded in 1829, and the events of the past still come back to remind students and faculty members of earlier days.

Most claims of paranormal activity are associated with Beecher Hall, a two-story building constructed in 1829. Witnesses claim to hear footsteps and the occasional moan. Years ago, Beecher Hall was a medical building, and cadavers were kept in the attic. There are several tales of people following the sound of footsteps up to the attic and then smelling the stench of decaying flesh.

The most famous spirit on campus is the so-called Gray Ghost. A female student climbing the curved staircase at the Alpha Phi Omega Hall claimed she saw a man in gray standing on the landing. She quickly realized he was not a student or a security officer—nor did he have a face. Several other students reported seeing a similar phantom over the next few years.

RHODE ISLAND'S SALVE REGINA UNIVERSITY

In 1999, a Newport, Rhode Island, writers' group was holding a conference at Salve Regina University's O'Hare Academic Center. Many guest writers had their books displayed for sale and multiple book signings were going on. One of the books on display was a slim volume of local ghost stories.

Campus security occasionally made rounds during this conference. At one point, a guard flipping through a book wondered aloud if there were any pictures of Salve's administrative building, Ochre Court, in it. He looked disappointed when someone told him there weren't any. He said Ochre Court was on his regular rounds and he had just returned from there after having witnessed some very "weird stuff."

When he was asked for details, he said that he'd had uncomfortable experiences there on several occasions and agreed to take some investigators who were at the conference with him to have a look for themselves. Two people accompanied him, one a paranormal investigator, the other an amateur, self-proclaimed medium.

It was dusk when they arrived at Ochre Court. The medium began talking about an angry spirit being present. She said he was an older man who was dressed in old-fashioned clothes. After they entered Ochre Court, the guard pointed to a closed door off the main hallway where he had heard footsteps. The door had slammed by itself. Suddenly, there was a shriek from the next room.

The guard and the investigator rushed into the entrance hall, where the medium stood in the middle of the floor, pointing at an oil portrait that hung to the right of the front entry. She was agitated and insisted she had seen the eyes of the man in the portrait following her. The guard suggested going down to the basement to explore some of the service tunnels beneath the mansion.

In the service corridors downstairs, double doors were propped open to reveal a wide hallway. As the three proceeded down the corridor, there were doors spaced at regular intervals, all of which were shut. The farther they went, the more agitated the medium became. After they passed the third closed door, her dismay became too much to ignore, and she declared she wouldn't take another step. The guard agreed. He and the medium turned and double-time marched back toward the stairs. The third investigator lingered for a moment, obviously reluctant to leave such a rare opportunity behind. The guard called for her to hurry, so she followed the others back toward the stairs. Just as she passed the double doors, both of them simultaneously and inexplicably clanged shut behind her with a deafening crash.

This incident can be very instructive when analyzed. It was not a controlled investigation; it was done spontaneously and it brought people with totally different investigative approaches together. What could have been a very productive investigation was cut short unnecessarily. The medium had no objectivity, and although there did seem to be evidence that some paranormal activity was taking place, she assumed too much from the start. This is a cautionary tale; this sort of thing should never happen on a serious investigation.

YORK, ENGLAND

York, England, is one of the most haunted places in all of Europe. It was inhabited by both the Romans and the Vikings, and as one of the most important cities in the British Empire, it has been the site of bloody battles and tragic deaths. At the Treasurer's House, weary Roman soldiers trudge through a basement, cut off at the knees. They are still following the original Roman road that lies beneath the building's foundations. The headless ghost of Thomas Percy, seventh Earl of Northumberland, roams the city, apparently searching for his severed head. He was beheaded in York for treason in 1572 after he led a plot against Elizabeth I.

The apparitions of two women and a child have been reported in a churchyard. One tale is that they are the ghosts of a mother, her child, and an abbess who were killed when Henry VIII's men occupied the church after the dissolution of the monasteries.

And then there are the children. The ghosts of countless children haunt the streets and buildings of York, crying for their mothers, begging for food, and grasping at tourists.

THE BORLEY RECTORY, ESSEX

The gloomy old building on the border between the counties of Suffolk and Essex has been described as the world's most haunted structure. Although the rectory itself was demolished in 1944 after being damaged in a fire five years earlier, its legends live on.

Poltergeist activity, full-body apparitions, disembodied voices, and ghostly chanting are associated with the rectory. Some claim that the spirits are those of a monk and a nun who were involved in a forbidden love affair. When they were found out, they suffered from the traditional punishment—the monk was decapitated, and the nun was buried alive.

During the fire, several witnesses claimed they saw a gray-clad nun slipping away from the inferno and a young girl standing at an upstairs window. When the ruins were excavated, a woman's skull and fragments of a skeleton were found buried several feet beneath the ground.

Theaters and Museums

Paranormal researchers have often noted that ghosts seem to be fond of theaters, as if they want to enact a drama without a final curtain for all eternity. The famous Adelphi Theatre in London is filled with ghostly activity, much of it attributed to the spirit of William Terriss, a popular actor who was murdered at the stage door in 1897.

Actors and patrons alike have heard mysterious tapping and footsteps running up the aisles and have watched stage settings being moved by invisible forces. Poltergeist activity has been reported, from flying cuff links in dressing rooms to cupboard doors springing open.

Actress Judy Carne claimed to have had an eerie encounter with an eighteenth-century actress who hanged herself in a dressing room. The spirit of the woman was often seen sitting alone in a balcony box. Carne told of a séance arranged to communicate with the phantom actress: "I tried to talk to her but the table we were sitting around rattled and I heard weeping."

THE HOLLYWOOD PANTAGES THEATRE

One of the last of the elaborate Hollywood movie palaces, the Pantages has been called one of the most beautiful theaters in the world. Eccentric billionaire Howard Hughes purchased the Pantages in 1949, but it fell into disrepair after he sold it. In 1967, Pacific Theatres bought the movie palace and restored it. Staff members who worked in the second-floor offices often reported feeling a presence, especially in the conference room, which had once been Hughes's office.

Karla Rubin, an executive assistant at the theater, stated that twice she caught sight of an apparition, a tall man dressed in modest business clothes. He has been glimpsed rounding a corner in the remodeled suite where Howard Hughes's original office door was once located.

THE BRITISH MUSEUM

Given the vast number of historical relics and ancient artifacts housed in the British Museum, it would be a surprise if the huge institution wasn't at least a *little* haunted. One of the most pervasive tales deals with the mummy of an Egyptian princess who was supposed to have lived in Thebes in 1600 B.C.E. Sneering at the possibility of a curse, an Egyptologist brought the princess's mummy and elaborate sarcophagus to England in 1910 and presented them to the British Museum.

Shortly afterward, the man's fortunes underwent a swift decline. A photographer who took pictures of the mummy immediately dropped dead of apparent heart failure. The curator in charge of the Egyptian exhibit was found dead in his bed. Several members of the museum staff reported seeing the figure of a woman floating through the halls.

THE RAILROADERS MEMORIAL MUSEUM

This museum in Altoona, Pennsylvania, has been the subject of several investigations over the years. Museum staff and visitors have reported sightings of ghosts in the building and around the site.

People have heard footsteps coming up behind them when no one is around and have reported harmless poltergeist activity in the museum gift shop. Several employees claimed to have seen a spirit-like figure climb over a steam locomotive exhibit engine only to vanish before it reached the other side. Many visitors reported catching a glimpse of a ghostly figure, freely moving about the outside of the engine.

One evening when a museum director entered an elevator, he saw a man standing in the rear, facing the back wall. The man turned to look over his shoulder at the director and then vanished. Shortly afterward, the director looked at a group photograph hanging on the wall of the first floor of the museum and recognized the man he had glimpsed in the elevator. The man's name was Frank, and he was a railroad worker who had been scalded to death by a broken steam valve. He was brought to the infirmary, where he died of his burns. He is now referred to as "Frank, the Friendly Central Pennsylvania Railroad Ghost."

Private Residences

Independent investigators should deal with clients as though they are interviewing witnesses to an accident. Although many levelheaded people claim to have seen ghosts, investigators should rule out all other possibilities and find out in a professional manner exactly what the claimants saw or heard.

For example, Chicago-area psychic researcher Norman Basile became involved in a mission to cleanse a haunted house in the suburb of St. Charles. After interviewing the residents of the house, Basile became personally affected by the sense of gloom that seemed to cling to the house and worried he was falling victim to the subject's delusions. He felt he had lost his sense of objectivity.

Taking photographs of the exterior of the house with infrared film, he noticed that faces appeared in the windows. "One showed a mysterious mist hanging over the whole house," he said.

Basile investigated the history of the house and found the site had been inhabited by Mound Builder Indians, a midwestern tribe who buried their dead in earthen mounds. Through his research, Basile identified several mounded areas that might have served as burial sites. He suspected that restless spirits resented the presence of the house.

Basile arranged for a cleansing ritual performed by Evelyn Paglini, a practicing Wiccan. Unfortunately, the owners of the home didn't fully cooperate with the terms of the ritual and the ghostly activity began anew.

Glossary

akashic records
The vast psychic record of all thoughts and emotions, some human, some not, that is sometimes accessible to advanced souls.

amulet
A symbolic magical object imbued with energy, meant to protect its wearer from harm; usually a necklace, ring, or pendant.

angel
A nonhuman entity; a winged celestial being, usually benevolent and kind and possessed of powers and knowledge beyond human comprehension.

anomaly
An occurrence for which there is seemingly no normal explanation.

apparition
The projection or manifestation of a paranormal being.

astral plane
A dimensional plane at a higher vibration than the earthly plane, where entities both good and bad can be encountered during astral travel in the astral body.

aura
An energy field that surrounds the physical body and is a reflection of the astral body, which can be influenced by thought and emotion.

banishing
A ceremonial, magical ritual to cast out negative energy and influences; it can refer either to a spiritual cleansing of a person or property, or to the closing of a magical rite.

cleansing
A ritual in which negative energy and entities are banished through prayers that are spoken aloud and may be adapted to the user's needs.

clearing
Synonym for *cleansing*.

demon
An evil, nonhuman entity.

dowsing
A means of locating different substances and energies by the means of two rods, which cross when the energy field that is being searched for is encountered.

ectoplasm
An ethereal substance that is supposedly exuded by the bodies of mediums and can form into objects and entities.

ectoplasmic mist
A substance that forms out of thin air and looks like a thick fog.

electronic voice phenomenon (EVP)
An utterance not heard as it is being spoken but audible later when the recording is played back.

electromagnetic field (EMF)
Electrical charges, found in varying degrees in anything that uses electricity or generates a magnetic field.

elemental
A nature spirit that can be either good or evil.

entity
A classification for a disembodied being, which may be a ghost, a spirit, an elemental, or a demon.

exorcism
A ritual performed to drive a devil or demon from the body or the house it is occupying.

ghost
A spirit that may or may not have been a living human being or animal and that can sometimes appear to be semitransparent.

haunting
The repeated appearance of ghosts, spirits, or poltergeists.

hypnosis
A state of altered consciousness, self-induced or created by an external agent. Franz Anton Mesmer first popularized this practice, which he called mesmerism.

instrumental transcommunication (ITC)
Two-way, real-time communication with spiritual beings. The entities provide advanced technical information through radio, television, telephones, and computers.

intelligent haunting
An entity that is aware of the presence of humans and may be interactive.

levitation
A rare phenomenon in which objects or persons are lifted or sometimes hurled through the air. Encountered occasionally in cases of poltergeist activity.

materialization
The brief physical appearance of an entity, seen as it is happening.

medium
A person with the ability to communicate with the dead; sometimes called a sensitive.

metaphysics
The school of philosophical thought that seeks to understand the meaning of existence and the human soul.

necromancy
The art and practice of communicating with the dead to obtain knowledge of the future or other hidden events.

poltergeist
The famous noisy ghost. A rare form of haunting wherein random objects are moved and sounds and speech are produced by unseen entities, which seems to crave attention and recognition. Frequently a child or adolescent is at the center of the phenomena.

provoking
A technique used by some investigators to anger spirits into responding or reacting.

psychokinesis
A paranormal phenomenon in which objects are moved solely by the powers of the psychic's mind. See *telekinesis*.

reincarnation
The belief that a soul will move on to another body after death to work out its karmic debt.

residual haunting
A psychic recording of an event that is traumatic or violent. It is repeated over and over; the entity involved does not interact with onlookers.

saging
See *smudge sticks.*

séance
The attempt by a group to contact the spirit world. A medium is usually the channel for the energies to manifest through.

sigil
A magical charm that forms an energy barrier and protective shield. It can be visualized or drawn.

sleep paralysis
A state between waking and sleep in which one is paralyzed and experiences a dark presence and/or feeling of oppression or suffocation.

smudge sticks
A Native American tool made of sage used for purification, healing, and cleansing ceremonies. The smoke is thought to clear negative energies.

spirit
A ghost; an entity that once existed on the earthly plane but has passed on.

synchronicity
Uncanny coincidences that seem too convenient to be truly coincidental.

telekinesis
The psychic phenomenon where objects are moved solely by the powers of the mind.

voice box
A device designed to allow communication with spirits through radio waves.

vortex
A rip in the fabric of space-time that opens into the spirit world and lets entities from the other side in.

ward
A magical construct that guards a person or a place.

wraith
The semitransparent image of a person that appears shortly before or after his or her death; also sometimes used when talking about a ghost.

Index